GW00382110

Time Management Teacher

How to be a great teacher whilst living a great life.

R.J. LEARNER

REAL WORLD BOOKS

Copyright © R.J. Learner 2020

The right of R.J. Learner to be identified as the
author of this work has been asserted by her in
accordance with the Copyright, Designs and Patents
Act 1988.

All rights reserved.

Cover image by Alfred Kenneally

No part of this publication may be reproduced, stored in a
retrieval system, or transmitted, in any form or by any
means, electronic, mechanical, photocopying, recording or
otherwise, without prior permission of the publishers.

This book is sold subject to the conditions that it shall not,
by way of trade or otherwise, be lent, re-sold, hired out or
otherwise circulated without the publisher's prior consent
in any form of binding or cover other than that in which it is
published and without a similar condition being imposed on
the subsequent purchaser.

ISBN: 9798665546391

Printed and bound in the EU

This book is dedicated to Jonathan, who told me to work smart and not hard not because he thought he knew better than me but because he thought I was better than I knew. He doesn't know it yet but he was the inspiration for both my career and 'Time Management Teacher'. It would not have been possible without his eternal patience, unwavering support and all-round good advice. I will always be grateful to him for both giving me the reason to have a life outside of work and the mindset to achieve it.

CONTENTS

PREFACE

I began writing this book in 2017 amid findings from the Office of National Statistics (OMS) that the risk of suicide among primary and nursery school teachers was nearly double patterns in the broader population of England. It is for those who work in profession with ever-changing demands and expectations, which, no matter how optimistic you are when you enter it, can and will eat you up and spit you out the other side. For people whose lives are hopelessly entangled with the profession and who watch with curiosity, then dread, as their more experienced peers who should be leading and inspiring them to new heights mysteriously descend into a pit of cynicism and incompetence.

Thankfully, this is not the inevitable consequence of dedicating your life to teaching. There is another way, which will endure beyond curriculum redesign or policy change, no matter what type of school you work in; it will not only enable you to survive with your professional dignity intact but will help you succeed, allowing you to leave the profession with the goal you sought to achieve when you went into it. Being a success in this profession is about more than meeting the teacher standards. It requires a fundamental mind shift in the way you view your professionalism and it ultimately comes down to decisions about how to manage your time. If you want to succeed in teaching, as with any endeavour, time isn't just the main thing to consider: it is the *only* thing. Yet this simple fact remains elusive within the very system designed to nurture us. Moreover, I have found that teachers – more so than other professionals – tend to approach the subject of 'time management' with more than a healthy degree of cynicism. Indeed, for most of my teaching career, that was how I approached the elusive subject. I have been in the position where I spent almost all my waking hours working and still never felt as if I could keep on top of it. Yet, still I was astounded when the senior leader conducting my professional development meeting concluded that I needed to 'learn to manage my time better' because (quite frankly) my excuses for not getting everything done properly were not good enough. I have to admit, I had naively expected some kind of praise for my valiant albeit failed efforts. After all, I had visibly put in the hours and tried as hard as I could to complete all of my roles. But unbeknownst to me, the institution which encouraged and perpetuated my inefficient behaviour had simultaneously placed the onus on me to find the means to improve it. As always, I was trying too hard to please and getting it all wrong. Ever the 'reflective practitioner', I began a diligent search for the solution everywhere my mind would take me. I asked my 'mentor'; consulted the deputy head and read countless books on the subject of teaching. Yet strangely, the outcome was always the same: that's just the way it is: you can't be an effective teacher *and* have time to spare. It seemed the only way out of the cycle was to learn to care less about outcomes or to persist in stoically 'trying my best' all the way out the back door. Perhaps the most lamentable example of this was when a deeply inspiring Head teacher I worked for raised a conciliatory hand to my shoulder and said, 'We're not moving mountains here.' She spoke with concern rather than condescension. I could see she was so swamped in red tape she could barely swivel her chair and yet she rehearsed the motions daily, with a serene smile on her face, simply doing what she could for the families of the pupils we taught. Her immaculate masquerade continued until one day the authorities got her and the executive head moved in. The removal of this layer of protection gave me the motivation I needed to continue the seemingly hopeless search. Amongst all the blind eyes and 'doing one's best', it is easy to lose sight of the fact that outcomes *always* matter and those at the head of the organisation will never lose sight of this bottom line. But are we lowly practitioners to be forgiven in the absence of any specific training in time management? Experience would say that such forgiveness - in the rare instances where it exists - is short-lived; and rightly so. The key to progression is to find a way to reconcile exceptional practice within the inadequate structure that exists - and ultimately to redesign what it means to teach, freeing the way for future generations.

Given the built-in failures of the system, it is unsurprising that the majority of teachers I have met along my career path have long-since conceded that their work load is impossible, reinforcing the assumption amongst the less experienced until it came to be accepted as fact. Maybe you too have almost resigned to the fact that working all the time and rarely feeling accomplished is normal; You may have come to believe that to have any kind of 'life' as a teacher that it is necessary to neglect key parts of your job. However, I can assume that your reading this alludes to a certain level of resistance to this assumption. Perhaps part of you knows that the adage: 'There aren't enough hours in the day', is too often used to justify a sub-standard breed of teaching, largely divorced from important outcomes. Maybe you too will identify with, whilst at the same time being at least mildly unsettled by the following example.

The insidiousness of the 'there aren't enough hours…' excuse came to my attention in 2018, when I made a formal complaint regarding the lack of marking at my eight-year-old's school and his (arguably) resultant lack of progress. In response I received an email from the 'Head of School' who promptly dismissed my preoccupation with my son's learning, explaining that marking was too time-consuming for teachers and it was better spent planning 'engaging' lessons rather than correcting work. To justify this comment, he added that in his own experience, students don't read teacher's comments and that when they do it can damage their self-esteem. After suppressing my immediate frustration with the general lack of outcome in this exchange, I was able to appreciate the significance of the letter. It was interesting on two counts: one that this policy-maker considered time to be so tight for teachers that they needed to choose between planning and marking and two: that this belief was so widely accepted that he felt confident enough to formalise it in an email to an already aggrieved parent. I struggled with whether the option to omit marking really was an informed decision rather than a retrospective excuse for failing to accomplish what he knew the teacher should have. I couldn't help but wonder whether if he might send a slightly altered version of the same letter to a parent complaining about the lack of variety in lessons, explaining that marking had in this case taken precedence. But ultimately this did not matter. How we respond to the problem boils down to the following question: Which facets of teaching are *really* important and how do we make the time to accomplish them within the time available? The question is an elephant in the room, becoming visible only when overtly asked. This book asks the elephant question multiple times in the hope through the discussion that ensues you will discover a practical answer which resonates with you.

INTRODUCTION

TIME TO TEACH EFFECTIVELY

'If you always do what you've always done, you'll always get
what you've always got.'
-     Henry Ford

It is the tendency in self-help literature to present such
solutions as a set of rules. However, as a fellow teacher,
you will understand that rules are made to be broken. I
will therefore use the more enduring currency of *principles*
in this book. Whilst you must constantly remind yourself
to follow rules, you apply principles automatically. The ten
principles of which the book is comprised have been
arranged in an order which felt natural to the author, based
loosely on the sequence in which she happened to acquire
them. Therefore it may serve you better to encounter the
principles in a different order and the book has been
arranged to facilitate this. The chapters have been labelled
as transparently as possible, to ensure you have the option
to read only what you wish to know. I know first-hand
that teachers are expected to suck more than enough well-
meaning eggs during their precious-little professional
development time. However, if you choose to read the
text through as a whole, it would be a privilege to share
with you my ungainly, yet luminous journey. I have tried
very hard not to come across as patronising but
unfortunately, when expounding what is ultimately
conventional wisdom, I may have at times failed in this
respect. It may help to think of this text as a recount of
my mistakes and my honest account of what I have
managed to learn from them. At times, my resulting
epiphanies may appear to you as nothing of the sort

1

because you learnt the lesson many moons ago - and at times you may share in my pain and understand precisely where I am coming from. It is my sincerest hope that occasionally, you will touch on something that helps you to reflect upon and improve your life as both a teacher and fellow human.

This book exists because for better or for worse, teaching is a profession unlike any other. The use of traditional time-management techniques do not apply in the same way as they would to administrative or other professional roles. To add to this, I have found that there is little sympathy for the teacher who works a mere thirty-nine weeks in the year and complains that he or she cannot cope with the workload. The principles outlined are essentially established time-management strategies adapted by the author to apply specifically to the teaching profession. To use your time to accomplish your craft, not someone else's bidding.

Implicit throughout is the assumption that *you are what you repeatedly do*. In other words, we can view almost everything we do as the result of habit. I appreciate that this is not a popular idea in the modern zeitgeist, particularly among teachers who, when it comes to the students at least, tend to maintain an almost obsessive preoccupation with 'choices'. However, I will attempt to prove that in order to embed the principles which will make a difference, at least a basic acceptance of the significance of habit formation is required. I can assume that if you have read this far, you already understand that a change in mind-set can transform any problem, however insurmountable it may seem. By working to reinforce the following principles, I hope that you will reclaim time to enjoy your life and pursue your personal goals.

Furthermore, I aim to prove that will help you to become a highly efficient and effective practitioner and those for reclaiming your free time are the very same. I sincerely hope you will conclude – through this book, or any other means - that neglecting parts of your job is as false a method of holding on to your time as ignoring a fine will help you to hold on to your money. You will ultimately steal from the future to pay the present.

As I suspect is the case for you, I have teachers for relatives and friends and can spot one a mile away. Perhaps like the builder's tan, we bare some outward sign of the trade, a kind of 'doormat' tattoo which marks the jovial acceptance of our perpetual state of working or feeling guilty about not working. I hope this book will help you to realise that what teachers do has no inherent connection with how we tend to do it. I invite you to work with me to untangle the real essence of the role from the system we have come to accept and ultimately to identify with a different class of teacher: the one who embraces teaching as a calling rather than a job. As Malcom Gladwell aptly puts it, a meaningful profession has three ingredients: 'Complexity; Autonomy, and Relationship between Effort and Reward'. This book is dedicated to the struggle involved in not allowing the first two to contradict the third.

PRINCIPLE ONE

GIVE YOUR WORK LESS ROOM

'The whole secret of a successful life is to find out what is one's destiny to do, and then do it.'

- Henry Ford

Gary Keller argues in *The One Thing* that the path to true happiness is to find your purpose and live in line with it. Happiness does not come as the result of success but happens on the way to fulfilment of one's purpose. In the rest of this book, I will outline the true purpose of teaching and labour the point that you must stay focussed on this purpose throughout the teaching day. But is teaching *your* purpose? The reason you believe you are here? More specifically, is your purpose and the source of your joy in helping others to experience success much like others have helped you to experience the same? Even if you cannot say an emphatic 'yes' to these questions, I would imagine I am safe in saying that if you are in the profession, it is not for the money (unless you know something I don't). This means that at least on some level you are motivated by something else which is inherent to the profession, be it a desire to improve the lives of your students or not.

However, I am going to hazard a guess that despite what your personal statement says, there are things in your life you consider even more important than this motivation. Most likely this involves family, pets, friends, travel, hopefully hobbies and perhaps your own learning or even another business. I don't know if there is something inherent in the profession which makes these things appear less important than the work we do, but I know from experience that students are often shocked to learn of teachers who had any sort of meaningful life outside the profession. And yet it is those things are what make you a real-life, 3-D person and ultimately a much more relatable and therefore effective teacher. Think about the teachers that influenced you the most in your life. Was it really those cardboard cut-outs which have faded to merge with grange-hill stereotypes of shoulder patches and socks with sandals? The ones we imagined were very lonely outside of school or was it the teacher with the tattoo he thought you didn't know about or the one who told you an off-the-record anecdote? Mine was the one who told me I would be a waitress for the rest of my life. Mr Vinton will stand immortal in those words for as long as I live. A very harsh but potentially true statement that he probably should never have made. An assertion that nonetheless changed my life and inspired me to start teaching.

Of course, I am not suggesting that you deliberately show off your belly piercing and share personal details with your students. Aside from this being unprofessional, it would likely come across as contrived and cringe-worthy to any self-respecting young person. However, if you prioritise life beyond work, then your overall attitude and range of interests will naturally come across in your style and manner with the students. If they see you as a learner, it serves to make their experience much less superficial and enables you to admit when you make mistakes and errors in judgement and demonstrate to the students how to learn from them. This begs the question of how to turn your noble 'live to work' ethic on its head. Ultimately, it comes down to a simple habit: if you want a life beyond your professional capacity, you need to prioritise principles that extend beyond your daily duties. Parkinson's Law is king here: it states that work expands to fill the time available. Therefore you need to give your give your work less room or it will expand to fill the time meant for fulfilling your life's purpose. In other words, get the things that really matter to you in order FIRST.

As important as your work is, any work you do for an employer should only fill one third of your life. Unfortunately, you will need to write another third off, as it is reserved for sleeping. This makes the remaining third all the more precious. This third of your life should be protected, first and foremost and time blocked before anything else. The most sensible way to do is this to ring-fence all your holiday days plus around half of your term-time weekends. Once this is done, then you can plan how you will use this time in the most productive way possible. This time is your 'life' in the elusive 'work/ life balance' - the time you need to make you a fulfilled human and it should be filled with your purpose.

Getting in Touch With your Purpose

On the hit American TV series Friends, loveable but dense character Joey comments innocently, "You don't have a TV?" and then after a pause, he adds, "What's all your furniture pointed at?" This is funny in part because it plays on the character's naïve way of looking at a set of circumstances which most of us take for granted. Joey takes the popular assumption that living rooms are for 'watching TV' to the extreme and turns it on its head, making the TV the very purpose for the living room and everything in it. In theory, Joey is making a more profound point: he is saying we should become more aware of the thing at which all our attention is focussed as we are passively declaring this is the most important thing in our lives. It is easy to rearrange the furniture - but first we need to have the perspective to see that it needs rearranging.

To learn what your purpose is, first you need to focus all your attention on what you think it is - then you will know if it's truly your purpose because of the unique way it makes you *feel*. You will know because each step you take on the journey to fulfilling your purpose will help you to experience joy. So try out working towards the purpose of teaching through the tasks that will help you to get there. If you feel a profound sense of joy - then you are on track to fulfilment. If it is not - you have learnt something valuable and it is time to find your new purpose. You need to both work and live on purpose. To give full attention to your purpose, there is no short cut for actively planning and earmarking your time. Just as you would during the school day.

You may feel that apportioning out each segment of your non-working time is excessive. After years of having a third party require it of you, you may have come to view the practice of scheduling as far too restrictive for your 'free' time. I can understand this. However, left to its own devices, this unplanned time gradually fills up with family or home-related chores, work related tasks and convalescence - which often involves television and sleep. However, without clear lines to demark when chores end and 'relaxation' begins, we will find we are often not fully present during any of this time. We effectively sleep-walk through our family time and zone out during our reflection time. We may not have even come to see this as a problem because our non-work time has – through the way we treat it - become less important than our work time, as though it doesn't matter if we have more or less of it, or if we waste it or not. First it is important to understand that a certain amount of relaxation is needed for us to even function in our professional capacity, but this should be seen as entirely separate from our 'life' time. Consider it in the same way as 'expenses' incurred on a work-related trip. In essence, recharging (i.e. switching off, 'zoning out', resting) for the purpose of doing more work is also part of 'work' time as it is a necessary consequence of the work. When considering 'work- life balance', work and the necessary convalesce time required to do it form work time and the remaining time is your 'life' time. As a teacher, you are likely to find that during term time (bar a few hours at the weekend), you exist in a perpetual cycle of work and convalesce. However, except in the case of modern slavery – where the worker is effectively 'owned' by the employer, the amount of hours spent on 'work' and 'life' are actually dictated by the owner of the 'life'. In other words: you need to decide how much time to spend at work and how much time to spend on life. Bear in mind, the less time spent on work, the less time which needs to be spent in convalescence, so it is in your best interests to keep this number as low as possible. The first step is to affect all of your power to reduce your working time to as close as possible to your minimal contracted hours. If you don't know what these are, make sure you refer to your contract to find out. There exists a lot of literature on what the appropriate balance for life is. I personally use bestselling author Jack Canfield's 'BALERT' system, which he describes in The Power of Focus which I thoroughly recommend you read. Whatever strategy you use, the important thing is that you learn to value and make productive use of your time outside of work. It is this time which will allow you to self-actualise your personal goals; in essence it is your 'life' and the time which you should value *most* of all. If you don't have an idea about what you want to do in this time, this is not an excuse to allow work to fill the time. In fact, it is a sure sign that you need to make time as soon as possible and then use it to REFLECT. As a matter of urgency even. 'Life' time should never be viewed as time to subsidise your work time. Teaching is a noble cause but are you literally willing to pay your life for it? You will never get your 'life' time back. What are your goals? Aspirations? What are you happy with or unhappy with? What are you going to do about it? To function as a human being, you need experience healthy relationships, physical and mental health, economic well-being, enjoyment, a sense of achievement and positive contribution. If any of these areas are being neglected, you seriously need to take a reality check and prioritise them. To make something a priority, you should be making progress towards it on a consistent and regular basis - ideally a small step each day. This is where the out of work scheduling comes into play. Remember: to prioritise is to diarise. For example, if you need to improve your relationships, schedule quality activities to invest in them a little each day. Much as you would embark on a Continued Professional Development course to help you support a pupil with a specific educational need, make it your business to learn about strategies to help you improve relationships through research, experts, courses or other strategies. If your relationships are unhealthy, a key place to start is reviewing the quality of communication which takes place within them. Communicating effectively needs to be actively learnt through strategies such as improving your empathetic listening skills. In order to say you value your health, you need review the amount of time you devote to this aspect. Are you earmarking time to research how this can be improved? Do you exercise daily? Drink the recommended amount of water? Eat a balanced diet? I may sound like a nag but if it is your reflex to refer to the stock answer 'I don't have time…' then you need to be aware you have paying for your work with your life. Literally. I'm just saying: if you are interested in time management, then extending your life would be the number one way to manage your time.

Your mental health is equally important. How do you feel about yourself? How comfortable are you that you are improving your sense of self and well-being? For example, if you want to look good - do something towards improving your appearance each day in the direction you want it to go. Apply a face cream or beauty treatment, choose your clothes carefully the night before. Don't underestimate the impact that applying deliberate improvement to even these small areas of your life can have. For example, upon being overlooked for promotions, I decided to follow the sage advice: dress for the job that you want, not the one you have. I changed my wardrobe to a more corporate style. I thoroughly committed as I was interested to see the impact, so I literally threw out all my clothes that did not conform to this style and I try each day to do something to improve the sharpness of my appearance. I haven't looked back since. Within months I noticed the impact, both in the way I was treated and the fact that others around me sharpened up too, creating a reflection of the action I had taken. Needless to say, I received the promotion but the most important change was to my sense of self. I treated myself with respect, which invited others to do so as well. Another area of your basic human functioning needs is your financial security. You may think that looking after your finances, is down to your pay-roll department and once you have secured your salary, no further action is required on your part. After all, you are paid to work and your pension is taken care of by your employer. However, it is important that you recognise the nature of the link between work and finance. If you had to perform a repetitive or menial job – let's say cleaning toilets - for which you would receive a certain amount of money for each number of toilets you cleaned or hours of your time spent cleaning toilets. The link between time and finance is straight-forward and simple to calculate. If you want more money, you clean more toilets (or spend more time doing so). If you want more time, you clean less toilets. However, for certain types of professional work, the link between time spent and money earned is much less straight-forward and for some teachers, barely exists at all. This is particularly dangerous because teachers will never earn more than they need to cover their basic requirements or what Herzberg would call 'hygiene factors'. As long as they do not experience economic distress, it is likely that they will barely notice how much they get paid. This is compounded by the fact that teachers will receive a retirement package as standard, so they feel less need to research the best forms of investment or give their life after teaching any kind of active thought. Economic success is a basic requirement and like all other aspects of your 'life' needs to exceed the bare minimum required to keep you able to work consistently. If your finances do not provide you and your family with future security, financial returns and a surplus to take part in life time experiences, they need your active attention. You need to build time to research the best financial opportunities and calculate how you can maximise your passive income.

You have the right to experience enjoyment and to feel that what you are doing matters. You need the time to reflect on what this is and ideally, you should make sure you are doing more of it than anything else. However, often people neglect 'life' priorities based on the assumption that a small amount of time available simply won't be enough to make a difference. This assumption is caused by the fact that it is more difficult to connect with and therefore believe in something which is not a current reality. You are not going to truly believe you can lose weight unless you are exercising or eating healthily right now. The more 'right now's you can create, and the more often the more it will become a reality in your mind until it comes to define you. It is the same with anything. You cannot honestly say you are a teacher if you have been out of the profession for ten years. You are what you do. So do it and it will be so. In using the time available to you now – however little of it you feel you have to spare – you will easily be able to find the motivation to create more time in which to do it. Don't fall for the common fallacy that motivation comes first. First, you have to give the motivation a reason to come.

Before you begin to invest time, it is important that you have a picture of what you want -the more specific, the better. This way your momentum towards your goal will be much faster and your time much better used in pursuit of it. However, you must be careful not to fall victim to present bias. We all have a tendency to get embroiled in what is happening right now and to favour it above what may happen in the future. It has evolutionary roots, stemming from the need to be hyper-aware of predators and immediate danger. This phenomenon, which is technically known as 'hyperbolic discounting' describes our tendency to perceive temporally distant events as 'smaller' than present ones. This feels natural to us because it *is*. It is our default setting. However, it is not this but our ability to override the system; to forgo present discomfort in order to avoid future catastrophe that has enabled us to inherit the earth. In a nut-shell; we have the ability to plan. We tend to use it too, as you are in taking the time to read this book rather than pursuing some other indulgent activity which may provide more immediate gratification. However, the very instant we are not mindful of it, our default settings will always take over, leading us to prioritise present events for no other reason than they are happening now and ignore potentially catastrophic future events which appear smaller simply because of their temporal distance. As the proverbial saying goes: *beware of distant elephants.*

If you are too exhausted by the grind of your daily life to consider the future, it is likely because you spend too much time worrying about things that don't matter. In the same way as you may eat foods that you know you shouldn't, you know as well as I do that there are staple non-negotiables that you should be spending your time and thoughts on but you don't. Chris Bailey in the 'Productivity project' hails the concept of 'hotspots' as an ideal way to ensure each area of your life is getting the time and attention it needs to enable you to have a balanced and fulfilled life. Hotspots are the areas of life to which you give the most importance: they are essentially your values. The idea is that each week, you reflect upon these areas to ensure you are giving them enough attention. Bailey tells us that whilst everyone loses sight of their values now and then, the most fulfilled and successful among us constantly 'correct course' ensure that the things which matter most are regularly brought back into focus. It goes without saying then that hotspots are unique to each person, as is the order in which they are ranked. However, there are a number of basic and essential facets of life which are rather curiously side-lined by those of us who choose to teach.

Namely:

1. Your health
2. Your relationships
3. Your finances
4. Your enjoyment and achievement
5. Your contribution to the world

Interestingly, we teachers already recognise these areas as essential facets of life. Just not *our* lives. We have sworn to protect them as the basic criteria to which every young person shall be entitled to work towards. You will probably recall the 'Every Child Matters' policy in which teachers are introduced to the SHEEP pledge – 'every child shall be: Safe, Healthy, Enjoy/Achieve, Economic (ally secure), (and make a) Positive contribution'. However, we can't really be expected to promote these principles in emerging adults if we don't consider them sacred in relation to ourselves. As has been the central theme of this book, to be effective at what we do, we need to start much closer to home. Remember Parkinson's Law? The rule of life that work spreads out to fill the time available to it. The reason work is spreading out is that YOU have given it free rein by not putting immovable priorities in place first. We need to put our work back its box until we have looked at what we should be prioritising in that space work is spreading out to fill.

Your Health

This is an easy one to start with; after all there is nothing more important than your health. It is obvious to us all that if one is you're not healthy then everything else lacks or is completely devoid of meaning. Or is it? Or is this irrefutable fact something we focus on only when there is a problem? If this is the case we need to step back: looking after your health should be a priority built in to the very fabric of your life in the form of healthy routines. What principles underlie your choices about what and when to eat? What does exercise mean to you? How do you invest in my mental and spiritual health? If your answers seem to conflict with what you know they should be, it is time to wake you're your health comes first and ideally you want to establish healthy routine which make it at the very least effortless or even enjoyable to take care of your health. A side effect of prioritising your health is more energy. You probably don't realise it but underlying feelings of guilt associated with not practising what you preach as well as the underlying worry linked to poor future health take up vast stores of mental energy. Knowing you have a good relationship with your health will be like getting a fresh new battery for your brain – it will function a lot more efficiently and last a heck of a lot longer.

Your Relationships

Healthy relationships are not an added extras. You need relationships to help you function in every aspect of your life. Perhaps it seems obvious to you. It should. Maintaining healthy relationships, like all other skills that lead to success need to be practised. You may find it comes naturally to you to have satisfying and productive relationships. Most likely you learnt this capacity from your interactions with your earliest caregivers (usually parents) and then you practiced in your early social relationships. If you did not learn from early misgivings, we exist in such large social groups these days that you were confronted with myriad opportunities to give you a second, third or fourth chance.

Sadly, for many, paid work can act as a kind of substitute for relationships; at least in the short term. Teaching seems to lend itself to this kind of misappropriation - primarily because as well as making you feel needed, it is potentially all-consuming. This allows it to fill any void left by a lack of a meaningful relationship. In extreme cases, relationships can be viewed as a hindrance, forcing you away from your work and making you feel guilty if you bring a pile of marking to the dinner table. When the relationship is gone, you can breathe a sigh of relief, knowing that you can work on your own schedule without being guilted into the restrictive framework of normal hours.

Yes I know; I've been there. It's not healthy.

When I say relationships, I don't mean any old relationship either. I'm talking about healthy two-way relationships. The kind that make you feel valued and happy when you think of them. The kind that need you to invest in yourself first so you can have something to bring to the party. The kind that it's not a chore to invest in but a joy. I can often be heard telling pupils that reading grows your brain and there is no such thing as 'wasted' reading but it is far more impactful when you read ever more deeply rather than simply sticking to what you know. A parallel can be drawn here with relationships - there is no such thing as wasted time spent nurturing relationships - the more you engage in deepening your understanding of relationships, the more you will grow your social capacity and therefore your ability to succeed as part of a *society*.

Sadly, relationships – even with the students and parents are often forgotten as we go about our business in educating children. Unfortunately, this situation could represent a grave misunderstanding of how we learn. Recent educational reform has presented our challenge as teachers to somehow 'get' an often reluctant majority of young people to produce specific outputs within a specified time frame. Fostering positive relationships with the students are viewed as a 'nice-to-have' extra but the main focus is on the output. But what if learning is actually a relational process? Humans have a certain edge over other animals due to not their larger brains or even greater intelligence, but to their unique capacity to collaborate on a grander scale than other species. We are more intelligent together. Trust between mentor and mentee is a crucial element of the learning process. If you are my mentor, it is essential that I listen to your advice, but it is just as crucial that you receive my response with empathy prior to issuing your next piece of advice. If this does not happen, the learning stops there. The education system as we know it today was originally born out of the need to nurture compliant citizens who can function within a system of clear boundaries like cogs in a machine.

I was in the supermarket the other day and the cashier, whilst mindlessly scanning my groceries was engaged in a conversation with his co-worker at another till. My cashier must have been the supervisor and the co-worker was negotiating at which time he should take his ten minute break considering another co-worker had just taken his ten minute break. Two things struck me about this exchange:

1. The level of discussion and seriousness involved in the negotiation

2. Both worker's apparent lack of awareness of the actual purpose of their job

Both 'boss' and 'worker' participated in their work mindlessly and automatically, only becoming engaged and animated when there was a chance for something for 'them'-however minor. I found it disturbing that the workers had been conditioned to such an extent that they could not have a ten-minute break without first negotiating it with their boss. They were concerned about the break and doing as they were told rather than being mindful of the activity in which they were engaged. But the more profoundly unsettling fact was they were probably so perfectly suited to this way of working because of their education. If they were to later find themselves in a job where they were expected to negotiate their own breaks and judge their own productivity, they would not have been prepared for this by what came before. A large bulk of our time is spent in explaining the output required and the exact conditions for production. We present ourselves, not as mentors or even fellow-humans but as the 'boss' and oracle of rights and wrongs. Is it any wonder that pupils come to us asking inane questions about whether or not they are allowed to use a particular writing instrument rather than requesting our professional opinion about the plausibility of this or that argument? Fostering a relationship of mutual trust facilitates a dialogue, which is the only way true learning can take place. A useful by product of approaching learning in this way is the time it saves you both in conflict and 'behaviour' management but also in giving explicit instructions and micromanaging responses to the point where you are doing all the work. If you find you often spend too much time 'talking' at the start of the lesson, looking at the trust which exists between you and your pupils may be the place to start.

Your Finances

As a public servant, you have likely been promised a degree of security and will have a modest pension for when you retire. However, this by no means implies that your finances are looked after. The way the pay structure is worked out, is so as to ensure the link between the work you do and the money you receive is virtually non-existent. Yes, you get paid, but as is the case with parenting, if you're in it for the money rather than some other source of intrinsic motivation, not only are you in the wrong job but you are suffering under a delusion. Let's not beat around the bush here, teachers are paid just enough as to prevent financial concerns inhibiting their ability to do their job – and sometimes not even that much. This is evident in the expectation of after school meetings, duties during lunchtime, and the implicit need to organise one's practise and workspace outside of designated hours. If you think about it, the divorce between hours spent and money received is inherent in the system. When considering your career options, you would have become aware that there are far more efficient ways to exchange your time for money. The school holidays, at least in theory, would provide more than adequate time to explore and manifest such options. However, the institution of teaching has in effect become a very sticky trap. Those outside of the profession view teachers much in the way that the working and middle classes view the very rich. They look with awe and wonder at the abundance of wealth before them and contemplate how they might better use the money if only it was available to them. In effect, we teachers have a much greater wealth than all the money in the world. We have time. More than a third if we protect our evenings and weekends. The non-teachers think about how they would use their time if they had so much of it. However, you and I know, all is not as it seems. For one thing, holidays are not paid time. Our pay does actually reflect hours spent. Calculate an hourly rate for yourself and you will see what I mean. Yet because we receive our monthly pay packet we get drawn into the illusion that all our time is paid for but we are given the gift of time off in the holidays. Then we fall down the slippery slope of feeling like we should be working all the time and luckily for our employer, there are always more jobs to be done. Interestingly, when it comes to the holidays and weekends, the jobs we end up doing - planning and marking - are the very ones which we should have completed during the time available at work. These are the key jobs for which we are paid. Why did we not get them done? We were dealing with a pastoral issue, planning a trip, setting up for the next lesson, doing lunch duty, taking part in a health and safety course, filling out an unnecessary form, speaking to a parent, answering emails, attending another meeting -you name it.

We get so drawn into the rhetoric of intrinsic motivation that we unwittingly spend our time diluting our modest hourly rate down to virtually nothing by spending evenings, weekends and school holidays on tasks related to the work or contemplating the same. We forget the relationship between hours and money and subsequently - forget to value our time. Essentially, we are committing the cardinal sin of living to work instead of working to live. The link between time and money is so much less explicit in teaching than in other types of employment. This will be most apparent to those for whom teaching is a second vocation. It certainly was for me at first, but I soon came to take it for granted. Teachers are expected to take on many more responsibilities than those which constitute part of the role and yet those which are primarily associated with the role, they do voluntarily, without thought about pay. If you think about it, if you

19

wanted to *make* money you would be spending as little time doing your job as possible. There are specific guidelines specifying the exact amount of non-contact time that each teacher should have and what your employer is not allowed to ask you to do within that time. Sadly, many teachers and employers are unaware of or simply ignore this advice, as the strength of the culture telling them 'that is just the way it is' is far stronger than the legislation. Whether we pay attention or not, the very fact that there needs to be such a legislative amount of 'protected time' at all speaks volumes about the way we view our occupation as distinct from pay. I track almost everything. I once showed my Headteacher my log of how much PPA time I had missed due to covering for staff absence or attending directed meetings during a specific half term. It had amounted to 23 hours. His reaction was interesting: it was one of shock and betrayal – what kind of person would even *think* like that? This was closely followed by defensiveness – when he launched into a rendition of 'If I documented the amount of time I spent...' Needless to say, he was much more mindful of 'protecting' my PPA time after that, sadly to the detriment of others within the organisation. After all, he was legally obliged. It is a frightening fact that if teachers kept it simple and were truly awake to the role for which they are paid, they would question almost all of what they spend their time doing. The remaining hours could be spent perfecting the skills which are linked to the job for which they are paid. In theory at least, given this time, they would ultimately become better teachers.

The first step to becoming financially healthy is to re-establish that long-severed link between money and time and come face to face with the uncomfortable reality that we ultimately sell our irreplaceable time for money. First you need to be mindful of what you give away in relation to the precise amount you get back. I would suggest keeping a simple time log on an excel spreadsheet. Log when you get to work and when you leave, time spent travelling to and from work and any time spent working at home. Then calculate the amount you are get paid per hour each day and over time. Subtract from this the money you spend on resources, subscriptions, motivational rewards for students etc. and don't claim back.

The reality check this give you will no doubt provide additional motivation for step two: do all you can to free yourself from the need to sell your time for money. Take some important time to work towards the surest path to becoming financially free: pay off your mortgage and establish a source of passive income to pay for your additional costs.

Essentially, you should keep in mind that however important your vocation makes you feel and how intrinsic your motivation is, until you are on the path to financial freedom, you are working class. Do yourself a favour and save the cavalier intrinsic motivation for when you are genuinely financially free. Until then, you should be keeping tabs on your hourly rate like work-shy 16 year old with a brand new National Insurance number.

If this is the first time you have considered your financial freedom, I would suggest aiming to protect your hours well beyond the recommended third of (let's face it) your life to enable you to spend us much hours on finance-generation as possible. Think of your teaching as a non-profit organisation. It is noble that you spend your hours contributing to its purpose and you should of course be compensated for those hours with somewhere to live and food to eat, but never tip the balance such that you are contributing your own funds to sustain it. The majority of your hours should be spent on investment in yourself - either in the other priority areas such as health or relationships or in endeavours which, unlike teaching, actually generate not only an income but a *profit*.

21

Your Enjoyment and Achievement

If the expectations are unmanageable or your boss is overbearing, remember: all of us have the right to enjoy what we do. Furthermore, if you are not enjoying your work – then something is wrong. This is so simple a fact that it is often overlooked by teachers and – perhaps unsurprisingly - by students. The reason is this so - called culture of immediate gratification (for which the youngest generation are commonly blamed). We teachers worked hard to achieve our QTS and anything else we have put our minds to and we understand the two fundamental rules about how life works. If you want something badly enough:

1. It can take a long time to achieve it
2. It isn't always going to be all fun and games

However, this supposition sometimes misses a vital presupposition. The first part: 'if you want something badly enough'. We forget a lot of the time that what we are asking the students to do is often something they don't want at all, let alone badly. Yes it is possible to encourage, cajole and incentivise but such extrinsic measures are not the most efficient means to achieve something. It's a bit like pushing a car to its destination – it's possible, and easier if you come at it from a number of different angles at once but of course the most efficient means is if you let the driver use his own energy. What you need is intrinsic motivation – then you don't even need to be there – unless their Satellite Navigation System is broken and then you can give them a map or a few directions and then they're off again! We get the enjoyment from first having the freedom to set our own goals. Enjoyment comes from the sense of purpose: from achieving something we set out to achieve, not from doing the bidding of another. This latter case simply provides initial relief from stress: *enjoyment* is very different. Enjoyment and a sense of ownership comes from autonomy. Understandably, the prospect of allowing students to have choice, causes anxiety amongst teachers. After all, certain things – such as exams - cannot be changed and these things by-and-large are not considered inherently enjoyable by students. However, that is not only the case with school – it is the case with life. Certain things are fixed such as bills and exams and other things are fluid – such as the way we respond to these things. It is not the job of the teacher to guide the student on their way towards these fixed mile-stones as though they are blind-folded but to encourage them to open their own eyes and decide how they want to proceed. Just as it is the student's right to feel a sense of enjoyment through achieving the things they want to achieve, it is yours also. You too must shake off the attitude of feeling like you have to and take pleasure in the choices you have before you. It is your choice how you approach what is fixed. Don't fall into the trap of prioritising doing as you are told before doing what you set out to do: teach.

Your Contribution to the World

Personal goals are essential for our sense of enjoyment and achievement and it is also our right to think more broadly and make a positive contribution to the world. There are a number of ways we could do this but the most obvious place to start is with your own career. It is likely that you began teaching with a somewhat modest goal. If you are like me, you will have turned to teaching because it was the only career that would pay you the salary you need for the hours that would fit around your life. The goal with which you started was to earn a certain amount and work certain hours. Well you achieved that first goal when you got the job. At that point, another goal was forced upon you:

achieve Qualified Teacher Status by successfully 'completing' your NQT phase. This 'goal' required a great deal of added stress for your mentor and one full day off a week. I don't know about you, but I found that to be the most unsatisfying goal I have ever achieved. I was more excited when I tied my shoelaces because at least when I was working towards that there was a period of genuine uncertainty - where I actually feared that perhaps I was destined to wear Velcro shoes for the rest of my life. There was also a sense of pride that was lacking in the NQT experience, for whilst I was able to reach my goal at age five, many of my peer group would struggle with this until age six or even seven. The NQT certificates on the other hand is more about paperwork and box ticking than anything else, and as long as you remain breathing for a year after your first job, you get signed off - earning you a modest pay rise and a certificate. This is what it must feel like for pupils when their teacher sets them a target. However, once this goal was achieved a window opened up for another goal. This was your chance. Did you set that next goal? Perhaps you had someone else's goals introduced to you at this point. Perhaps the Headteacher thought you'd make a fine subject or Phase leader? At this point, you may have found your career going in a certain direction. Did you stop and ask yourself: "What's the outcome *I* want?" If you are currently at that stage, you should ask yourself this question. If you really do want to change outcomes for the school then that is fantastic. Clarify those outcomes and give them a time frame and by all means take on the additional responsibility as an opportunity to realise your vision. However, when you achieve the goal that you set, make sure you recognise the window and set a new goal. Your day-to-day practice should be a reflection of *your* purpose. Your goals should lead you to a decisive outcome and the principle underling them should sit right alongside educating. If you are taking on the additional responsibility for some extraneous reason such as: a sense of obligation, extra money or additional non-contact time, you should consider whether or not:

a)   The desired outcome is a reality. For example, the non-contact time could soon get eaten up with the responsibility itself and is in my experience, a precarious resource in some schools for which you must constantly fight to retain.

b)   Whether or not his outcome is worthy of sitting beside the purpose of your job as a teacher: i.e. enabling children to learn. Could you comfortably say that the purpose of your main job is to enable learning and the purpose of your additional responsibility (which is supposed to be a step up) is to reduce your contact time with the pupils?

If your answer to *a)* and *b)* are no, then you should firmly abstain from accepting the responsibility. Be honest about your reasons and explain that you would like to focus on the tasks that fulfil the purpose of your actual job! Your line manager should respect you for showing such a dedicated understanding the purpose of your job. They should respect you even more when you set and meet targets that relate to this, such as raising attainment to some reasonable standard which you will be able to do easily, given that your work time is dedicated to this purpose, especially if you use a forum such as a Professional Development Meeting to do this. Your next step is to create a big vision representing the culmination of all the things you want to achieve through your work which may see you as an award-winning practitioner, consultant, Headteacher, or even proprietor of your very own school. This is important because when you reach it, you'll know that you're done. That's when the retirement plans come in. It may sound ironic but when talking about career goals, you should begin with this end in mind. When I talk about retirement, I'm not talking about a little portion of life left after the government decide you're too old to do your job any more. I'm talking about your next challenge after you have given your very best effort to teaching and achieved your long-term vision. Ideally, this portion of time will coincide with financial freedom which will open out yet more opportunities for you to make a difference. This is not about counting down the days like a prisoner awaiting release. This is about doing what you want to do and getting the heck out of there - onto the next thing - always working towards more effective impact and those things that bring you happiness and satisfaction. As Jack Canfield says, "Make it clear why you are here" then set about dedicating your time to only those things that bring you closer to this purpose. If you are to make a positive contribution, you need to retain your autonomy and gather the means to sustain it. Don't fall prey to doing as you are told; first intend and then set out to do as you intended.

Defining Your Purpose

To live by your purpose, you need two things:

- A vision of your best self
- A set of guiding principles

Fortunately, these things are self-reinforcing and are essentially one and the same. If you find it daunting to conjure up a vision from scratch, I would suggest that you start with the principles. After you have reviewed the key areas of your life as outlined above, you will find that you naturally begin to outline principles as you go along and you should write these down, they are essentially your 'rules for life' and will apply at all times. They will be things like: 'always choose the lower calorie option when given two choices of snack' or 'always pay ten percent of earnings into your bank account as soon as you get paid'. Of course there will be times when you don't follow these principles, but these occasions will be exceptional and the principle will still endure in your mind, helpfully guiding you to make the right choice next time. These principles will guide you towards your purpose, by helping you to visualise what you will become if you consistently follow your principles. To develop your vision, use the areas of your life that you value as a starting point. Start with those identified above. Then begin to set out your guiding principles in these areas. Now imagine how your life would be if you consistently followed these principles. This is your *vision*. Alternatively, you can start with the ideal vision of your life and try to work backwards to the principles that you would need to get there.

Repeat this simple process for each of the areas you value until they are covered:

- Values
- Principles
- Vision

The final step is to try to combine all your visions into a single vision. The easiest way to do this is by creating a vision board. This could be as simple as a collage of pictures representing your vision about each of the key areas but there are a number of ways to identify with all your visions at once such as a painting or piece of creative writing. The main thing is that you create a tangible representation of your ideas which you can review regularly and hold in your mind to help you focus.

Give Your Work Time 'Hard Edges'

The next step is to clearly recognise the time you sell you your employer as just that: time sold. Then you need to draw a box around your contracted working hours in a thick proverbial marker pen. The time that you sell to your employer is an essential part of your fulfilling your purpose. For one thing, it can give you the funding needed to establish financial security. It will also allow you to contribute to the world through fulfilling your 'big' work goals. That time is precious and important but one thing it is not is infinite. Like anything in life, you have to know how much enough is and stop there or over-selling your time will become a harmful addition like over-spending or alcoholism. Over-selling your time to your employer devalues your time and this diminishes the impact you can have in that time. It is colloquially known as 'workaholism' but I suggest you rename it as 'over-selling' your time so that you can keep in mind what is truly at stake. As I outlined at the start of this chapter, when you over-sell your time, you are essentially agreeing to sell part of your most valuable and irreplaceable asset at bargain basement prices. Try to keep in mind the big picture: your time is for one thing – fulfilling your life's purpose – not for selling.

It may help you to draw the metaphorical lines I mentioned as physical lines in your diary. Then make it a principle not to step outside of these lines unless absolutely necessary.

All Time Was Not Created Equal

Through the process of putting your work on hold and getting in touch with your true priorities, you will come to the realisation that all time is not created equal. This can be a profound and enlightening prospect; whilst time spend on productive work can feel satisfying and can make you feel good, the time spent in line with your true purpose and nature as a human: your health; relationships;

your quest for enjoyment; achievement; financial freedom and to make a difference to the world will bring you a feeling of peace beyond compare. Once you get a taste of using your time in this way, it will affect the way you view all your choices from then on.

When my son was eight, I had a leadership job which required both teaching and management time but without the actual time to do both. This is a prospect that many of you reading this can probably identify with. As is often the case in the teaching profession, a great portion of the work ended up taking place largely outside of school hours. This put me in a perpetual state of fear at the prospect of getting behind. Of course, I didn't complain because that would make me appear incompetent. My son had his school assembly on the Friday which was an INSET day for my school. I weighed up the potential long-term impact of attending the 'essential' training against the prospect of attending the assembly. As I have explained, once ingrained, it is much harder to break a habit than continue with it – even when more effort is required to complete the habitual action. I had habitually ignored invitations to my child's assemblies his whole life, just as I had habitually attended all work commitments even under extenuating circumstances. However, on this occasion, I had recently reviewed my principles, and going against all my urges, I decided to request the morning off to attend his assembly. Earlier that week, my son has been ill and rather than allow this to hinder my work, he had been passed from relatives to friends whilst I had attempted to arrange medical appointments and worried from my classroom. It had worked out OK but I couldn't shake off the subconscious guilt stemming from the fact that I was ignoring my values. The decision was a pivotal moment for me. My son's response to seeing me was priceless: having never made it to one of these occasions, I had no idea how important it was to have your mum at school

29

when you're eight. Having naively thought he might even be embarrassed to have me there, I was bowled over by his open and genuine appreciation of my decision to spend 20 minutes of my day in his world. When I later caught up with the webinar that my colleagues had watched that morning, I found it interesting and professionally stimulating to a degree. But I did not get the feeling that it resonated with my purpose in any sense. That was the missing ingredient. I had swapped one activity which on the surface would have appeared compulsory in order to choose an activity which was wholly voluntary and yet I was assured that I had made the right choice: in this case, doing as I was told was not the right thing to do. The activity I had chosen offered vastly more value for the time I spent on it, simply because it was in line with my purpose. Even without clearly identifying your purpose, you will probably have some inkling as to what it is as your principles will allude to it. It will be the thing your mind drifts to in a stressful or boring situation; the only thing that will fill you with energy when you are exhausted. This for me was spending quality time with my son to help him grow into a well-adjusted human being. The great news is, once you have explicitly identified your purpose and set out to achieve it, your mind will not allow you to focus unless you are on-course to achieving it: it will become easy not just to work on purpose but to *live* on purpose.

The remaining chapters of this book will help you to focus in on your 'work box'. The box that represents a third of your limited time on this planet. I made this chapter the longest and placed it first to give you the opportunity to clarify what you really want before you read on. As they say, before you climb the ladder, first make sure it's up against the right wall. If it is your purpose in life to enable others to learn, then teach you must - and don't allow anything to distract you from the necessary tasks that will enable you to fulfil that end. The remainder of this book will identify 9 principles for rearranging your 'work box' to keep you on task.

To give you an idea, of what to expect - a much shorter (and arguably more efficient) version of this book would go like this:

If you want to be an excellent teacher (but also want a happier life) follow these 5 steps:

1. *Decide on your life's purpose.*
2. *Go to work early.*
3. *Spend your time planning, teaching and giving feedback.*
4. *Say no to everything else.*
5. *Go home early.*
6. *Fulfil your life's purpose.*

The end.

The version I hope you are about to read is a tad longer – but sometimes it is necessary to wade through the woods before you can reach clarity. I invite you to come to the woods with me to discover the principles which could save your life – quite literally – by allowing your work to stay in its box whilst at the same time becoming the most efficient teacher you can possibly be.

FINISHED IS BETTER THAN PERFECT

PRINCIPLE TWO

FINISHED IS BETTER THAN PERFECT

'You can't build a reputation on what you are *going* to do.'

- Henry Ford

L et us begin with the elephant in the room. The assumption that the tasks of which teaching is composed are infinite and therefore inherently *impossible* to complete. As the best time management experts will tell you: effective time management begins with the acceptance that *there will never be enough time to complete everything*. The advice is usually 'draw a line under it and leave it alone now; its home time'. To know when enough is enough. In a well-meaning pledge to obtain the elusive 'work-life balance' we let ourselves and each other 'off the hook' when things are not completed to a certain standard.

However, the detrimental effects of constantly 'letting yourself off the hook' are dangerously subtle. One of which is a special breed of exhaustion known as *decision fatigue*. When you finish work - after being kicked out by the cleaner or falling asleep in your pile of marking – you will have been forcibly evicted from the task. However, mentally you are still working on it. You never consciously closed the loop and the processing will persist indefinitely in the background. If you overload your brain with items to process, it will slow everything down, potentially leading to a crash. This is because, generally speaking, our brains are no good at recall. If you don't 'capture' an idea in a place that your brain can trust, it will work overtime to remember it. Whilst you may forget the specific action you need to complete, there will always be a tiny part of your brain holding you accountable for it. Have you ever walked into or out of the room with that feeling that you should be doing something but you can't quite remember what it is? Isn't it an uncomfortable feeling? In all likelihood the task itself wasn't important – it just felt that way because it was using so much of your energy. It's your brain's way of reverse-justifying it's overspending. This is why if you say to yourself: 'Ah well if it was important, I would remember it', you will usually find that the feeling dissipates somewhat. However, if you are new to the habit of closure, you are likely carrying a number of these tasks in your mind, unaware of their impact. These undone tasks are using valuable attention units which drain your mental battery and impair your focus and ability to fully relax. Think of it as though each task you have to complete is an open tab on a laptop. As long as the tab is open, it is draining energy from the machine. The more tabs we have open, the more quickly this happens. When the battery is nearing empty, the machine operates less efficiently, making it more difficult to complete the open tasks. In this situation, we have three choices:

1. Continue to use the laptop in the same way, allowing it to crash (and potentially lose your work).
2. Stop using the computer and plug it in to recharge fully before attempting to use it again.
3. Save and close each of the open tabs, choosing only one task to complete at a time. This way you can continue to work whilst the battery charges.

The pursuit of the 'work life balance' might encourage you to choose option two. To translate the metaphor –the decision leave the work for a sustained period in order to rest and 'recharge' levels of mental energy is referred to as 'escapism'. It may at times feel as though you have no other choice due to the sheer impossibility of completing all the tasks. Most often, 'escapism' seems to be the only way to evade the constant hum of mental noise created by the incomplete tasks. The reason this approach often doesn't work is because we actually *gain* energy by stemming the flow of waste each time a task is completed. This allows the energy used to constantly process it can be reserved for better uses.

However, we can get so used to leaving our jobs 'unfinished' that even the most experienced teacher may struggle to even recognise when the job is 'done'. A painter knows when he is finished because the room has been painted, a mechanic when the car is fixed. Even the surgeon or lawyer can rely on patients treated or cases solved. But when has the teacher completed his or her job? Thankfully, the job of teaching is no more impossible to complete than this book is impossible to read. Granted, you could always read the book again or understand it better but you are very clear about the difference between having finished reading a book and not having finished a book. We could say that reading a single book could be an infinite journey of mastery and complexity as we turn the pages back and forth in a fervour.

Or we could systematically read one page at a time until we have read the last and then proclaim to have finished the book.

At first it may feel as though reading a book is far simpler than teaching. However, there are an infinite number of elements involved in anything we do. The more we break any task down, the more complex it seems. The only way we can get closure is by viewing it in a way which gives us a kind of modular sense of completion. In the case of reading, through practise we have developed a sequence of automatic habits which free us from needing to give energy to every single element of the task. As a result, we have learnt what it feels like to have accomplished the task. So whilst picking up the habit may at first have been a cognitive load, it is now really easy to see the end. What you refer to as your 'job' is a collection of tasks which you complete cyclically over a given time period: lessons, weekdays, weeks, terms etc. In an ideal world, the central authority will issue the objectives, you will turn these into schemes of work; teach them; assess the outcomes and then begin the cycle again. Reading a book requires reading and turning the page and repeating this process until there are no more pages to read. Teaching requires planning and preparation, teaching, assessment and feedback and repeating this process until all the objectives are met. You can experience a feeling of completion at the end of each stage of the cycle; when each cycle is completed and when all the objectives are met. So why don't we ever feel like we have finished our work?

Chances are you view this 'big picture' approach as overly simplistic. You can't just say: today I will plan, teach and assess and that's it because you are not in charge of the vast majority of what happens each day. The majority of what you spend your time doing cannot be predicted as the day begins. You have to take each event and task as it comes and deal with it all like tennis balls firing from a machine. At the start of the day you have your plans and the balls start coming. At first, you can catch them and bat away any you can't. However, as your energy lags, you begin to miss the odd ball and they end up in the corner of the room somewhere. To make matters worse, your tasks will be coming from numerous sources aside from your pupils and before long, you are not only exhausted by batting balls all day, you have to face the prospect of looking behind you and clearing up all the balls you missed during the day. It is no wonder that you feel swamped by the end of the first day of term and surely you can be forgiven for leaving a few balls behind to clear up tomorrow. However, you now have less energy to deal with the now more numerous tasks you have to deal with the next day – as you begin with balls on the floor.

It would be very easy for me to say that any tasks outside of your priorities should be side-lined or ignored. However, I appreciate that much of what we deal with will be linked to pupils' safety or assigned to us by senior staff. You are expected to plan in detail every minute of the working day, prepare, make, collect and purchase resources to use, and to mark, present and display all of the fruits of their labour all before the following day when the cycle begins again. On top of this, there are longer term commitments such as clubs, parents' evenings and enrichment events to prepare for, reports to write and data to analyse and this is not to mention making time for continued professional development. All of this admin would sound like a dream if teachers had a thirty hour work week to complete it in but of course they only really have the two and a half hours per week allowed for non-contact time. The rest of the time, they must teach and are at the mercy of constant interruptions from pupils and often their parents who have their own sometimes widely varying agendas. These responsibilities form the unwritten priorities of your job: keep the children safe and the 'powers that be' happy. If you fail at either of these, your days are numbered no matter how well the children score on their standardised assessments. If this is your situation, you are a custodian first, appeaser second, teacher third. Besides, once a task has been assigned, it begins to drain our mental resources and ignoring it will only make matters worse. This interesting phenomenon is known as 'The Zeigarnik effect' and it relates to the tendency for the brain to remember uncompleted tasks over those which have been completed.

I used to think multitasking was the answer; marking books from the previous lesson whilst 'teaching' the next.

The more tasks on the go at once, the more effective I felt I was being. This was before I realised what was actually happening in my brain when I did this. According to time management expert Dave Crenshaw, what we are really doing when we try to multitask is 'switch tasking', which entails rapidly changing gears from one task to another. He highlights how counter-productive this approach is given that even the most complex computer program is incapable of doing two things at once. The resultant mistakes and lack of recall mean it takes significantly longer to accomplish each task than if it had been given the full quota of attention available to it. In an article for the Harvard Business Review, Peter Bregman found that productivity is reduced by 40% when we attempt to multitask. Furthermore, Crenshaw warns that this habit not only diminishes concentration but also depletes our reserves of will-power by forcing us to make more decisions than we would otherwise need to. He explains that the brain has different 'channels', each of which requires it to process information in a different way. If you are attempting to complete two mindful tasks using different channels simultaneously, you will find that much of the time and energy spent on the tasks is spent on changing channels. Each time you change channels to revisit the task at hand, you need to activate the rules of that channel which means that very little time and energy remains to make progress on the tasks at hand. Switch tasking causes you to lose minutes here and there, looking back at something to check, processing something that you didn't process the first time and searching frantically for lost items. It also causes stress which diminishes energy and motivation which are best reserved for completing your most important tasks. I should acknowledge here that one specific form of multitasking can actually be used to improve concentration. This is where you use an additional open channel to complete a compatible activity which will support the completion of the main task.

However, such multi-channel multitasking only works if you are experienced enough at one of the activities to allow 'auto-pilot' to take over and you chose two compatible activities. You can do two things at once, sure, but it is actually impossible to *focus* on two tasks at once. For example, you may have found that listening to non-lyrical music or other soothing sounds such as a candle or rain can help you to focus on creative tasks such as planning or writing reports. You have probably also noticed the opposite can be true with lyrical music. This is because the words in the music will compete for your attention with the words you want to write. The lyrics and words for writing require the same brain channel and therefore both pieces of content cannot be acknowledged at once. Conversely, if the task is creative, rather than linguistic in nature, then lyrics can appear to support your activity. Other tasks such as walking whilst thinking through a lesson plan or driving whilst listening to some relevant CDP material work also well in combination. If you consider how channels work, you can use them to your advantage but, alas, they cannot be used for getting more done during a given time slot, only for getting *one* task done more efficiently.

Sadly, you may have come to the conclusion that switching tasks constantly throughout the day is an inevitable consequence of having a job with a number of different layers to it. It's a bit like comparing someone trying to lose weight through overeating to a drug addict attempting to get clean. Both are foul to addictive and habitual behaviour so it may be tempting to prescribe the same cure but you can't. Why? The drug addict can go cold turkey and relocate so he/she is no longer surrounded by the negative substance, whereas if the dieter does this, he/she knows she will *die*. In a similar way, the teacher is surrounded by a multitude of different tasks to complete and the temptation to multitask may never go away. That is unless you discover another way to cope with the situation. Thankfully, as we shall discuss in Principle Seven, there is a way to achieve more tasks within a specified period. It is a strategic method whereby you do not *switch* frantically between tasks but you classify and *batch* them.

However, before you are ready to batch effectively, you need to live by the principle of getting tasks finished which is at the heart of the strategy. As counter-initiative as it may sound, the fastest way to complete multiple tasks is to get in the habit of focussing on each task separately and to complete it before beginning the next. This enables you to keep the metaphorical laptop charged and to attempt each task with all the energy available, closing it neatly when finished but remaining fully present and in control. Seth Godin refers to the concept of closure as 'shipping' and he argues it is the single most important factor in determining your success. You need to retrain yourself to reach a state of conclusion for each task you encounter. Don't expect this to be obvious at first – you will need to think hard to identify the specific action required to give you that feeling of closure. It might be as straight-forward as writing a follow-up email or as obscure as making an apology. So why isn't this practise a natural part of our lives? I suspect this is because it is often uncomfortable. As you probably know full-well, in times of anxiety, we tend to choose what is easy over what is right. All too often, deadlines can be extended or even ignored. If our brains have learnt not to expect closure, we may not seek it and would not realise that it is linked to the resulting feelings of 'unfinishedness'. However, when you apply this principle, you will certainly feel the positive effects in the somewhat surprising form of increase in energy and attention.

So how do we calm the background noise? The solution is simple and potentially life-changing: every single thought to which an action is required needs to be captured in an acceptable place that you know you will be able to find it later. We have already established that your brain is not a suitable place for storing such things as it is not so good at recall - so we need to move to a capturing system. This can take many forms but a simple version can be created using four items you already use to some extent:

- A planner - a traditional diary is not necessary: a calendar and a notebook or their digital equivalents are all that are required.
- An in-tray
- A filing system (a filing cabinet with hanging files is best for this)
- Label-making stationery (an automatic label-maker with extra labels and batteries is ideal but some white sticky labels and a decent pen will suffice).

Now you have gathered your equipment, you will need to get your capture system ready to use. The first thing you need to do is make sure all the things you have yet to decide an action about are in one place so you can process them. This includes un-marked work, materials from the TES you intend to read one day, even staple guns without staples. In fact, every item which is not in its proper place should be in the in-tray. Now at first, you are likely to have more items than could possibly fit in a regular-sized in-tray. That's ok, gather them anyway and just place them beside it. If you have a pigeon hole, empty that into your in tray as well. Make a game of it if you like. The one important thing to remember is DON'T LEAVE ANYTHING OUT. The only things left behind should be things that are in their proper place. If in doubt, put it in the tray. If it is too big, scribble a note about it on a scrap of paper and place this in your in tray.

Now, if you are anything like I was, you will also be

collecting unprocessed emails in your digital inbox. Both your digital inbox and your physical inbox will need to be cleared but you can leave them there for now. Finally, you will need to empty the in-tray in your head. You know: that space in your brain where you store all the ideas and promises you have yet to write down. The contents of the mental in-tray need to be placed with all the others so they can be sorted. To do this, you will need a pile of post-its (or scrap paper) and a pen. Write down anything on your mind. You will find that ideas in your head are likely to require an action and you should try to write the action required rather than just the item wherever possible. For example: instead of 'flowerpots' write 'find three flowerpots' (a bit like a smart target). Using one post-it or leaf of paper for each item (you will see why this is important later). They do not need to be work-related items such as 'mark year 8 assignments'. They could be mundane items like 'buy pasta' or 'book dentist appointment' or even vague or outlandish ideas such as 'research holiday destinations'. The important thing is that, like with the physical in tray, you don't leave anything out. Keep going until you can't think of anything else. That doesn't mean you are in a zen-like state without thoughts, but so that your mind is still enough that you can focus one thing without a 'that reminds me' thought busting in on you for a while. I realise at first this may seem like a daunting, even unthinkable prospect, having effectively a large pile of junk sitting in front of you. Even once you are finished it, your mind will probably be screaming, "What have I done?" But I need you to trust me on this: you will feel a uniquely positive feeling. Try to remember that all that stuff existed anyway, not being done, just now it is all in one place so you can confront it and deal with it. Once this is done, you will likely never have to repeat this process again, because your mind will constantly nag you to get back to that feeling.

Now you will need a block of uninterrupted time to

deal with all of your unprocessed material. Just this once, clearing out your in-trays is going to take a long time-the best part of a day depending on the number of unprocessed items in your life. I would recommend coming into school for one full day towards the beginning of the holidays, or at the weekend to do this as you will want to do it in one go.

Now you are ready to process. To be clear, processing is not about completing tasks. It is about deciding what you will do and when about ideas that require an action and storing or disposing of items which do not currently need an action. The reason that unfinished tasks create that uncomfortable feeling is not because they are unfinished. It is simply because you haven't properly decided what to do about them and when. A part of your mind is unwilling to let go of them which is what gives you that nagging feeling telling you that you need to be doing something. It may be comforting to hear that we are able to cope perfectly well with unfinished tasks, as long as they are processed and we can trust ourselves to get them done. Self-esteem is a reflection of our ability to trust ourselves. If you are constantly letting yourself down, you won't trust yourself, which is why your brain will work overtime trying to remind you of tasks you haven't finished - it simply doesn't trust you to get them done. The irony is, all that cerebral background noise is a major reason you can't focus and complete your most important tasks. Effective processing is the only way to break the cycle. The processing routine is a simple one. First you will need to select an item from the in-tray. Then you decide what, if anything needs to be done. There are two types of item in this world: Those which require action and those which don't. We will deal first with those items which require some kind of action. Decide when it will get done and record this decision in your capturing system. Then you move on to the next item and repeat the process. Each time you select an item, you have a decision to make: do it, delegate it or defer it. With any item that needs processing the '3D' question is the first question you should ask.

Can I: Do it now? Delegate it? Defer it?

Do It Now

This only applies if you are dealing with an urgent or a priority task. If you are anything like I was, you may find yourself completing non-urgent, non-priority tasks right away. Usually because you think if you don't complete right there and then, you will forget about it and it will later become a priority. You must remember: if it is not important now, it is not likely to become so at any point. Try to keep in mind that your business is only with the important stuff: your priorities. Putting things into your system will take a small amount of time and you must weigh that time against the length of the task if you are to be most efficient. If it is an urgent or priority task, and will take you less than three minutes to complete, then do so right away. Otherwise, you will need to select from one of the other options. You may be familiar with the sage advice 'touch it once!' This golden rule reminds you to process items as soon as you encounter them, rather than the habit that many of us have of putting them to one side to deal with 'later'-an infamous time that often doesn't come. Do you throw away your junk mail as soon as you lay your hands on it? Do you immediately set a calendar or task reminder to pay bills and then file the letters? Do you photograph all fliers and leaflets and file them in your electronic notebook before throwing them away? If not, get into the habit of constantly reminding yourself to 'touch it once'. Once you have decided it is important or urgent enough to complete now - you should consider whether or not you can do it in less time than it takes to defer or delegate it.

Delegate It

If you are not in a management role, you may feel uncomfortable with the idea of delegating tasks. Particularly if you are well-practised in your profession and have developed efficient and exacting methods for completing your work. But the principle of delegation refers not to these aspects of your job which you are your priorities, but all the other minutia which can get in the way. Strictly speaking, you shouldn't be spending your time completing tasks for which you are not specifically being paid or are not good at (or both). I used to think that only people who are full of themselves delegated tasks to others. However, I now realise you need to have humility to delegate effectively. It takes both a leap of faith and an understanding that you are not the best at every single job to outsource. If you're lucky enough to have a teaching assistant, look at them carefully - I guarantee they are better than you and many of the tasks you insist on doing yourself. If you don't have a teaching assistant - which is increasingly the case, you will always have a class full of students whom can be considered a little army of apprentices. They will both learn from you, and enjoy assisting you. In all cases of delegation, time and training at the beginning, use find yourself free for the job. Don't be afraid that they won't get it right first time. They won't but don't give up. Their making mistakes is a crucial part of becoming your apprentice. As long as you're honest with them, they will learn what you expect and so will you. Even if you decide to take back the task, you have broken it down to my simple form and your find that it takes you less time to complete as a result.

Defer It

You may find that the deference option the hardest to

stick to. It's because if you would like me you avoid procrastination and to all intents and purposes, this is a type of procrastination (albeit on purpose). However, we must remember our focus is on the important task. It is very likely that in the process of processing we will come across tasks which are urgent to someone else but which are neither urgent nor important to us. To give you an example: Imagine you are in the process of going through your in-tray and you come across a post-it. It is a message from a parent asking you if you could please find Johnny's gym bag. As a competent adult you could probably locate Johnny's gym bag - perhaps even fairly quickly. But of course the question is not if you can but whether you *should*. Even if you found the bag within 10 minutes (which strikes me as super-efficient), you must think about what lesson you could've planned or taught, or what helpful feedback you could've given to students in that time. The truth is, if you leave the problem alone for long enough - it will solve itself. The gym bag has not evaporated and it will show up. Perhaps even teaching Johnny (and his mother) a little lesson about responsibility if it takes longer than expected to find. Many problems solve themselves when treated in this way. On the problem of Johnny's gym bag I would suggest expending no energy at all. However if you must expend energy, I would suggest keeping it to a minimum. Write a note on the board about the gym bag, or delegate it to a reliable student. Better yet - if you must do something - catch Johnny himself and tell him about his mother's message.

Ditch It

There is always a fourth option, one which is used far less often than perhaps it should: *ditch it*. This is by far the most cathartic and efficient option but it is seldom used. Why? The answer is the reason most people don't take the action they know they should: fear. Fear of regret, fear of having it play on their mind or other consequences. There will always be consequences for every action and every non-action. The important thing to remember is there are often invisible consequences for taking actions which outweigh those of the consequences you are attempting to avoid by carrying out the action. Every choice is a choice *not* to do something else. For example, I choose to respond to an email from my boss asking for some data which you have already sent. This will keep her happy and make me appear useful and dedicated to my job. This sounds fair enough. It only takes ten minutes in clock time to locate the data and respond sufficiently to the email. However, are you aware that that the ten minutes was borrowed from you planning, teaching and feedback time? Did you actually consent to this reduction to your PPA? Losing this time will ultimately cause you to take the time out of family time, relaxation time or time spent working on your own projects or detract from your effectiveness as a teacher. All of which I can imagine will have further reaching consequences than not responding to the email. You probably think that ten minutes of your time is not bad for the return that you will get. However, as we shall consider in later chapters, ten minutes clock time can be worth far more than you may think. Another reason to think carefully before saying 'yes' is that doing so automatically puts you in the frame of mind to say yes to other similar tasks throughout the day. It is a slippery slope. I would suggest you always step back and think before completing a task that someone else has put on your agenda. If you are new to saying 'no', I would recommend going cold turkey at first to realign your mind-set with your priorities. It can help to view every 'yes' is a 'no' to something else. Alarmingly, many of the tasks we say 'yes' to have nominal consequences compared to the high priority tasks we are turning down by default. In the data scenario your boss will - of course - get her data and will very quickly forget she even asked you for it. If she doesn't she will probably feel bad for having asked as you are clearly too busy - in which case she will think twice before asking you a second time. However, if she does harass you again - I should imagine she has some control issues which would indicate an unhealthy relationship between you.

This is the real meaning behind the sage advice 'we can't do it all'. No, we cannot literally do all actions but the thing is – we really don't *need* to do all actions. This doesn't entail that we can't do all the actions required to complete our job. It's simply a case of being very clear about which actions need to be done to complete our job compared with those which at best make very little difference at all and at worst set us back from doing what is necessary.

So how to identify your priorities? One simple means of doing so is the use of a priority device such as the Eisenhower decision matrix (*figure 1*.). The matrix consists of four quadrants: important, not important, urgent and not urgent and any 'to do' task can be placed somewhere on the matrix. If you take the time to use one of these devices, you will be able to see as Eisenhower warns that tasks which are important (priorities) are actually seldom urgent. This means that they demand comparably little attention from us when they turn up and we tend to leave them uncompleted. Likewise, tasks which are deemed 'urgent' are seldom important. We spend most of our time completing non-priority tasks simply because they arrive in our inboxes as shouting, thrashing emergencies. When you deal with these tasks, you often find yourself in a frantic cycle of fire-fighting. Before you even consider any item for processing you should ask yourself: "what does this mean to me?" In the following section, you will learn that if it is a priority it should be obvious because it will be linked to the purpose of your job (or your life). If it is not in this category then at the processing stage you will need to delegate, defer or ditch it.

	Urgent	Not Urgent
Important	**DO IT NOW**	**PLAN IT** Schedule a time to do it
Not Important	**DELEGATE IT** Who can do it for you?	**DROP IT** Eliminate it

Figure 1. Eisenhower Decision Matrix

Using a To-Do List

If an item is not ditched at first sight, it needs to go into a 'to-do' list. In all likelihood you are already practised at using one of these. They are viewed as something that most 'organised' people use but they are actually seen as highly controversial in the productivity world. This is largely because studies tend to show that the majority of items remain undone on to do lists, suggesting they are not as practical as they may at first appear. The Zeigarnik affect tells us that the undone tasks can cause a permanent drain on our attention. However, the use of lists is not entirely misguided as they can be used effectively. Writing a list can provide relief in times of stress because it calms the cerebral noise created by our nagging thoughts. Humans tend to have a bias towards action and many of the thoughts which flow through our minds trigger a desire to carry out a resultant action. However, we are only capable of carrying out one action at a time and our ability to complete that particular action is hindered if we are entertaining thoughts of other actions at the same time. Writing the action on a list captures the idea outside of our short-term memory and gives the mind a sense of peace. However this experience can be very brief if we do not act on the item within a certain amount of time of adding it to the list, after which time it begins nagging again and continues to drain our mental energy. Moreover, if we have multiple lists of this type, it is tantamount to having multiple windows open on a device and will drain our energy even faster. If we placed the item on the list, it follows that at some point we intended to complete it. Why, then, do list items remain unaddressed? Some of the possible reasons will be addressed below.

The items don't seem as urgent as what you are doing right now

This phenomenon is known as 'Present Bias'. It was illustrated famously in the 'marshmallow test' of the late 1960s and early 1970s led by psychologist Walter Mischel that we have a tendency to prioritize what we think and feel now over the feelings of our future selves. The test was designed to see how children responded when offered a single marshmallow now or two later. It was found that the children who showed more will-power and were able to delay gratification tended to experience greater future success. It is a fallacy to follow instinct when it is leading us to place a greater bias on something in the present simply because it is in the present rather than the future. It is important to look after the interests of your future self, rather than making them clean up your messes.

The reason you put the item there no longer exists (or they are there without good reason)

Once you get the hang of deliberate deference as described in 'defer it' above, you will find that a surprising amount of the time, problems solve themselves. You see no logical reason to return to these items because they are no longer presenting as issues, but you must. If they persist on the list they are still acting like open tabs and draining your energy for no good reason. You must delete them!

You don't have the resources you need to hand when it comes to completing them

This is a common reason for not completing tasks. We tend to think it is justifiable to not complete a task because we do not have some essential permission/ piece of equipment - you name it. However the real problem is not that we don't have something we are waiting on but that we have put the wrong thing on the list. If you have put on the list: 'print off timetable' and the printer is out of ink and paper and is not connected to the network, then you have bigger problems to add to your list before you can begin. Our brains have a habit of skipping ahead to a future step when we have an outcome in mind, which means we grossly underestimate the number of steps involved in completing even a simple task. If you don't have time to complete all the necessary steps prior to completing the task in mind, then you will need to return to the drawing board, but at least the process of considering the *real* next move will help you to make an informed decision. If you do need to use another printer, then having this idea in mind is a necessary first step or strangely, this obvious solution may elude you and force you into inaction.

You have not identified the next action for the task, or done so specifically enough

If you ever find yourself procrastinating about a certain item on your list, it is very likely that the problem is you haven't specifically identified the next action needed to complete the task. This can make the task much more daunting to complete, which is another reason tasks remain uncompleted. Specifying the exact next move required to achieve your desired end at the moment of capturing saves you valuable attention units in deciding this at the moment of action and takes away the subconscious drag associated with the task.

The rules for using a list

You should always use more than one list and aim to clear it. One way to organise items is according to mind-set and location. This way you will always have to hand the necessary resources to complete a specific task. Categories such as 'at computer' and 'not at computer' can be especially helpful, as you will save time assessing whether or not you have the tools to complete the tasks before you attempt to do so. In theory, you should be able to compete the 'in classroom' list from start to finish when you are in the 'classroom', without any consideration for the order in which to complete the tasks. I have a list for less than five minute tasks which I complete in queues or when waiting for meetings. You will need to try different categories of list for yourself and you will often find that many of the categories are unnecessary. Keep updating your system with the aim of keeping it as simple as possible. To begin with, I would advise having a 'waiting on' list for items you have delegated as this will help you to chase them up. It should be reviewed as regularly as you need to stop you feeling that panicky cluttered feeling. I would recommend a 'deferred' list in which to store items which have spent too long on your list but which you still consider important. However, you should be brutal when you complete your review. If you not doing it has had few consequences up until now, consider ditching or at the very least delegating the item to get it out of your system. Items which have a particular time and date should be placed in the calendar and deleted from the list.

Make sure you always have your list to hand. At any one time it should represent a complete inventory of all the tasks you need to complete in all the areas of your life. Again, I recommend using a digital notebook as this makes it easier to delete and move items to different lists according to a change in priorities. Each time you complete a task, delete the item from your list and decide what if any next action needs to be completed. You can then complete another item in your list. Present bias tends to lead us to complete the items that we perceive to be quick and easy. These so-called 'quick wins' can give us a boost of energy which feels great and for this reason, they are often hailed by time-management experts as a great remedy for lack of motivation. Beware. It is easy to get hooked on the feeling it gives you which can cause you to lose sight of why we are working to begin with. Remember: work is supposed to have a purpose, not to be pursued for its own sake. In reality, these quick wins are likely to be low priority tasks which, if you are not careful can end up on your list just for the sake of your being able to cross them off. You should look to complete the most important task at any given time, ideally aiming to ensure that your list of to do items are *all* important, having delegated, deferred, done or ditched any other items. Next, you allocate times in the day when you will be working from your list, and blocks of time where you will not. Whilst getting stuff done feels amazing, the whole of life is not composed of actions. It is all about balance - an ample amount of thinking, acting and communicating. When we are acting, we intend to limit thinking and communication to the absolute minimum but it is not realistic or desirable to do this at all times. If we try to do this at all times, the thinking and chatting will eventually creep in and spoil the action anyway so it isn't really a choice. At the beginning, we talked about the two types of item that will arrive in your in tray. Those which require action and those which do not. Now let's discuss those items which do not require an action. These are otherwise known as reference materials. If you are not sure what constitutes a reference material - it is a thing you will need at a later date. If you are highly unlikely to need it, consider ditching it or storing it in some form in your digital filing system. If you won't need it, the action is obvious: bin it. If it is easily accessible from the internet, bin it. You can easily find it again if you need it. Your reference materials should be stored in one of two places: a physical filing system or your digital notebook.

A Digital Notebook

The digital filing system should be your first port of call. There are two types of item that should be stored in the digital notebook:

- To-do items
- Reference materials

To do items have already been covered in the previous section so this section will discuss how to store reference materials in your digital notebook. Digital notebook software is free and can be used to share files across a range of devices. You can download apps easily to your smartphone which is the most effective way to use the software. The most popular notebook for this purpose is Evernote. I use Microsoft OneNote as this comes with my Microsoft package. You can open a notebook for storing work-based documents and one for personal documents. To be honest, it doesn't really matter how you arrange the documents as they can easily be moved about and you can use a search engine to retrieve them easily. Store them under whatever heading comes to mind naturally. I would recommend storing each item as a separate page as this means files can easily be deleted when no longer required or reorganised as needed. Original documents can be scanned or simply photographed using your camera phone. The originals must then be discarded or stored in a physical filing system on the rare occasion that the item is considered irreplaceable (e.g. birth certificates or passports).

A Physical Filing System

Your physical filing system is going out of date. It is only necessary because you live in a transitory period in time where physical has only partially been replaced by digital. People still believe there is a choice to be made between the two, but really it is becoming obvious that the use of paper as a means of communication is wasteful, inefficient and unnecessary. Nonetheless, it is essential we have one in place simply to cope with the last of the remaining dinosaurs - much like the human cashier for those who fear the self-service till. Unlike the digital notebook, it doesn't deal efficiently with to-do items and these will need to be stored in a paper notebook. It isn't portable and therefore will need to have a counterpart for household and personal items in a different location. Worst of all, it doesn't have a built in search engine and therefore should be as simple and intuitive as possible. I will suggest the following steps to set one up and would recommend doing so at the earliest possibility:

1. Buy (or reclaim) a filing cabinet with at least two drawers and a working lock.

2. Obtain some hanging folders, file folders and a label maker.

3. Label a hanging folder for each pupil you teach.

That's it. The files you have set up for each pupil will be used to collect samples of work and assessment data. It will prove indispensable for those impromptu meetings where specific questions catch you on the hop and proves much easier to keep and locate than separate files stored in different places. Obviously it is important that the cabinet can be locked.

The other drawer will be used to store everything else. You will file as you go. Labelling files with a logical and intuitive name (i.e. the first thing that comes to mind) will help you to locate them easily. It also helps to slide the files in alphabetical order. Make sure you keep lots of spare batteries, label refills, files and folders close to hand - ideally in another drawer. This is essential if you intend on keeping your system in operation. Primarily because as you run out of items you will need to run around finding them at inopportune moments. This wastes time and disrupts flow. More damagingly, when things run out: it is annoying and over time this negative association will cause a subconscious resistance to the activity of filing. Once it ceases to be fun and satisfying, you will stop doing it. It's simply a question of when! That's why I insist on the use of the label-maker. There is something inherently satisfying about using one and this serves as the 'reward' in the habit loop for many people. We will discuss this more in later chapters but if you have ever used a label-maker, you probably know what I mean!

Principle Two has been all about the practical task of prioritising completed actions over intentions and getting things done. We discussed the Zeigarnik effect caused by leaving tasks uncompleted and considered why the work-life balance we seek remains elusive. We explored what 'finished' feels like and established that the key to calming the Zeigarnik beast is to establish it all the time. We looked at importance of offering our full attention to important tasks and a practical means of establishing our priorities and ensuring these get completed. The main principle is that thoughts need to be processed and completed. Once you have set up your system, and cleared out your mind, you will be able to see clearly what is truly important. You're a teacher, so you already know that it leads to results when you set out your intentions before you begin a task so that you know when they are met. So ask yourself whether you have been able to identify your ultimate smart target:

What is the purpose of your job?

FINISHED IS BETTER THAN PERFECT

PRINCIPLE THREE

WORK ON PURPOSE

'It's what a thing actually does that matters, not what it's
supposed to do.'

- Henry Ford

In 1998, a little-known team of rowers came second to last - again. They should have come to accept that they simply weren't good enough and like so many of us, got back in the game and tried harder. But this team were different; they were not prepared to work harder, they wanted to work *smarter*. By 2000, Ben Hunt-Davis and his team had not only improved their performance: they won the first Olympic Gold Medal to have been won by a British crew since 1912. How did this happen? In a complete mind-set overhaul, Ben Hunt-Davis had decided to try out a tactic so simple, he wondered why it hadn't been obvious before. It went like this: prior to any action any member of the team performed, they would ask themselves, "Will it make the boat go faster?" If the answer was 'yes', then the action would take place. If the answer was 'no', it did not. It may sound simplistic but it is based on the principle that success is nothing more than focussing on your purpose and nothing else. It is called the law of 'incremental gains'; the principle that it's the little things you do each day which truly make the difference, not the rarer grand gestures which we tend to over-focus on when reverse-engineering success. Quite literally: you are what you do each day. Which begs the question: do you like what you do each day? More importantly, is it who you are? Because it should be.

59

We spend far too much of our time, energy and money on things that simply don't matter thus depleting reserves for things that do. There are more than enough resources for us to achieve our desired ends but we squander them before we get to the point of deciding what actually matters and what doesn't. Yes you fill your days (and nights and weekends) with all the things teachers are supposed to do - but did you ever sit down and ask - is this actually *relevant* to what I'm trying to achieve?

If I'd been born one hundred years ago, perhaps I would have gone about my teaching business being sexist, elitist and dictatorial. I might have humiliated and beaten children and - supposing I were a woman - not taken a husband because that was what teachers did back then. I could have argued I doing as I was expected to do but would that make it any less morally wrong (and on some counts indicative of psychopathy)? More pertinent is the question of whether any of it actually made me a better teacher. Hopefully you can pat yourself on the back for not doing any of the above in your career thus far. But was it really an intentional choice? Or do you simply find yourself just as much a victim of circumstance and doing whatever it is you do simply because that is what you presume teachers do? I'm not saying that in 100 years teachers of the day will look back at your actions and judgementally ask – "how *could* you?" But we can never say never.

The 'Perato Principle' is hailed by time-management experts as a golden rule. It is sometimes known as the law of the vital few and tells us that only a small proportion of the actions we complete (20% to be approximate) dictate the majority (80%) of the results we experience. In other words, the vast majority of tasks we complete make only the smallest amount of difference to our lives. This effect was initially discovered in economics, in the finding that approximately 20% of people own 80% of the wealth, but has been repeated with an eerie level of consistency in enough arenas to be generally accepted as an unwritten rule of life. If all tasks were not created equally, then logic tells us we need to move towards spending our valuable time completing the tasks which make the greatest impact on fulfilling our intended purpose. Yes, the other 80% of tasks may lead to some benefit, but only a comparably small amount. We are better off ditching these where possible and spending the time we would have spent on them completing tasks which will have a greater impact. So if the choice is between completing an administrative exercise whilst the child completes their work and giving the student some valuable feedback as they complete their work, where the time spent doing these is equal, then the logical choice for a teacher would be to give the feedback. In Principle Two we touched on why people focus so much on the inane, often at the expense of what is really important. The most likely reason is that focussing on purpose requires the kind of deep thinking that only those who have mastered the art of quieting the daily noise of our busy lives are capable of doing. And now hopefully that includes you. It will make the boat go faster to choose the feedback option whilst the administrative exercise may make you feel as though you are 'getting things done'. Therein lies the important difference between being busy and being productive - it all comes down to having the purpose at the forefront of your mind at all times. Cal Newport in his best-selling book 'Deep Work' advises always looking at the bigger picture and adopting what he calls the 'craftsman approach' to tool selection. Suppose you are like many people and rely on having your own vehicle to commute to and from work and to complete various chores. You could use public transport but would rather not have the stress, inconvenience or additional cost attached to this means of transport. Take the choice between owning and leasing a car. Most people choose to own their car because it has some well-known benefits such as not having to make regular payments to the lease company and being able to sell it should you want or need to. We look for benefits in a specific choice and once we see that there are some, we tend to assume that the choice is worth our time. This approach is known as the 'any-benefit' approach and is the one which many of us adopt unquestioningly in most of our actions. However, when you look more carefully at this situation you will realise that the 'any-benefit' approach ignores the fact that the negative effects can far outweigh any positive effects. In the lease example, if one were to add up the cost of depreciation, MOTs and increased expenditure on repairs on a car one owns, then they would equal or even outweigh the cost of a lease. This is before you add up the cost of interest accrued through loans or hire-purchase agreements prior to the car being fully paid off or any non-financial costs such as stress and inconvenience. All things considered, the lease car best fulfils the purpose of getting to and from work without stress, inconvenience and additional costs and is therefore the best tool for the job. Now you have considered all options, you have chosen the 'craftsman approach' to decision making and selected consciously with the purpose in mind.

So what is the purpose of your job? It is important that we first distinguish between the role of a teacher and the *purpose* for which the role exists. The role will vary dependant on circumstance, whilst the purpose is constant and eternal. Just as the purpose of a waiter is not to serve tables but to ensure the food is served, the purpose of a teacher is not to 'teach' but to *ensure learning takes place*. Whilst other means may be found to ensure food is served (such as self-service kiosks) or to ensure people learn (reading for example), the need for learning to take place will persist and it is at the heart of what teaching is about and why it exists to begin with. So if the purpose is to ensure learning takes place, then what is our role as a twenty-first-century teacher in ensuring that happens?

Of all the teaching tasks I mentioned earlier, spanning administrator through to social worker, it might surprise you to find that only three are essential to the job you been employed to do. In theory, you should be able to list these of the tip of your tongue but in all likelihood, no one made them explicit during your teacher training or at any time thereafter. If they ever did, it is likely that you have become far too bogged down to remember them. If you apply the 'craftsman approach' to teaching then you would select the following tools to do your job:

1. Planning
2. Teaching
3. Feedback

That's it. For teachers, "Will it make the boat go faster?" means: "Will it help the pupils to better meet their learning outcomes?" These tasks are the three to which the answer is most definitely yes. So many of us lose sight of these priorities and borrow time from these sacrosanct areas to feed the other menial monsters that plague our teaching lives. To put it plainly, if you are not planning, teaching and providing feedback, you are not doing your job. Moreover, these three activities are cyclical in nature, with each feeding into the other. If one area is ineffective, the others follow suit. As we shall discuss in more depth in the next three sections, if your planning is poor, it will affect your teaching. If your teaching is poor, then this puts more pressure on your marking. If your marking is poor, it will not inform your planning, and so the cycle continues. Together they add up to a single thing - which after all is the true meaning of the word *priority*: teaching.

Priority One: Planning

63

Benjamin Franklin said, "Fail to prepare and you are preparing to fail." In no profession is this truer than teaching. Your planning time is where you troubleshoot and see the bigger picture. It enables you to make the most effective use of your time but ironically often becomes one of the things that teachers fail to do on the grounds of not having the time. In 'The Seven Habits of Highly Effective People' Covey tells the story of a woodcutter spending hours attempting to fell a tree. When someone advises the woodcutter to take five minutes out to sharpen his saw, reassuring him that many more hours of work will be saved by accomplishing this comparably simple task. The woodcutter looks at him as though he were mad and could not see that he did not have time to sharpen his saw because he was so frantically busy trying to cut down the tree. Teachers sharpen our saws by planning, enabling us to use our time more effectively. We are expected to plan on three levels: long term, medium term and short term and are officially given a modest 2.5 hours per week to complete this enormous task. Unsurprisingly, the vast majority of teachers complete their planning outside of this time, finding the allocated PPA time consumed with putting out fires, completing tasks delegated to them by someone else or being eaten away by time-thieves. In Principle Ten: *making each minute count*, I will discuss some useful methods of how to combat these issues but the crux of the problem is that once the planning task is started, it frequently takes far longer than the time allowed. The trouble is your brain remembers this feeling and learns to prefer tasks that feel easy to finish. Therefore, when a task feels insurmountable it is rarely completed. Remember from the previous chapter, that whatever lies your intuitive brain is telling you, *done is better than perfect.* Later on I will explain how you can use the time allotted for tasks more efficiently to ensure that your planning not only gets done but that it *serves* you and saves you time as a result. Interestingly, whilst there are a number of excellent resource-sharing websites available for teachers, I would not advise simply downloading ready-made plans from websites. It is not the planning of what exact content you will teach that is key to serving you but *how* and *when* you will teach it that is key. In the next section, we will look in more detail at the type of lessons we should be planning for if we are serious about serving the purpose of teaching.

Priority Two: Teaching

Unlike planning and marking, teaching is not something we can put to one side and decide *not* to do. As an SLT member, I used to say: 'If you want an accurate predictor of how well a set of pupils' will do in a particular subject, then look at their timetable; the amount of face-to-face time dedicated to that area of their learning will give you an idea of how well they will do.' This is true to an extent but too often lesson time is spent with our students sitting there passively, waiting for our carefully prepared resources to be passed around or displayed on a screen; waiting to receive our instructions before 'learning' begins. If we don't have anything planned, we have to think of something because whether we teach or not, the pupils are there and they need to be managed and their needs attended to. This can be an exhausting practice: once the input is finished, the questions begin. If you have ever spent twenty minutes setting a class to work on a task and ended up with a queue of pupils at your desk with a range of queries ranging from the irrelevant, "Can I go to the toilet?" to the infuriating "I'm finished". The inspectors would prefer us to be actively teaching the entire lesson, and to be honest, we conclude, this seems to be the only way to ensure the work is of sufficient quality. So we take ourselves to sit with a group or indulge in the practice of 'circulating' the room, checking over shoulders to ensure work is completed and putting out fires as they arise by darting from raised hand to raised hand.

Alternatively, we give the pupils a task to complete which is easy enough that they will need minimal or no support to complete it. This way, we will not be disturbed as often and can get on with something else. The small problem with this is that by not challenging your students, you are not enabling learning to take place and therefore you are not doing your job. In fact you are doing the *opposite* of your job. So what is the answer? If we actively teach, we can't do two thirds of our job, yet if we actively *don't* teach we are not doing the one third of our job that gives the other two meaning. The answer to this conundrum, like with most problems, entails a change in *mind-set*. It can help to think of teaching as the act of facilitating learning. If the learning is facilitated well, then it is not necessary for the teacher to work so hard. In fact, I would argue that the less time a teacher spends actively instructing pupils, the richer and faster their learning will be. It seems the key to effective teaching, as with all things, is to work smart not hard.

Instead of the scenarios depicted above, picture this scenario: You set the pupils to work and they decide on their task, the success criteria and the timeframe. If they come across a problem, they don't come to you, but have at their disposal a wide range of trouble-shooting methods far better than any assistance you can provide. Because they are responsible for the task and the criteria against which the output will be measured, the learning behaviour is also managed by the students themselves. You are in the background, modelling efficient methods of working by doing so *yourself*. Matching your tasks with their tasks. When the students are required to collaborate, collaborate with some of them to create a lesson plan or some other task which will benefit you equally. When they are expected to read - you read. When they are writing, you write too. When they share work, you share work. If you mark, they mark and so on.

When the work is finished, it is presented to an audience, who provide directed improvement comments which outweigh any feedback you could offer. The students take on board the suggestions and make faster progress than ever and you can spend the time marking the books as the comments are made or you could instruct the pupils to note down their own feedback, freeing you up to prepare the next stage of learning, informed by the formative assessment as it takes place. The scenario described requires a very particular driving force in order to work. A force which you may doubt exists in a high enough quantity to make any of the above seem possible: internal motivation. So much of the literature on education is about teachers motivating students. In my opinion this is nonsense. I would go so far as to say it is impossible to motivate anyone apart from yourself. Motivation can inspire the same in others, but it is not something you *do* to someone else. If we think we can motivate others, we are at risk of creating a culture of 'curling kids' whereby we work overtime to sweep away all of the barriers to learning in order to allow pupils to slide effortlessly towards *our* goals. However, if we can allow the children to see and take ownership of their goals, they will make their own way towards them. We will find we need to step out of the way whilst they remove their own barriers or maybe even work alongside them under their instruction.

Now of course, this scenario requires prior investment. You need to buy into the principles of Carol Dweck's *growth mind-set* to understand that teaching the pupils to troubleshoot for themselves creates resilient, independent learners. You have to first train the children to this new way of working and some will take longer than others to receive it. However, you will probably find it is your highest attaining pupils that struggle at first, as you will have freed your less able pupils from constantly banging up against their inadequacies and enabled them to focus on their strengths. They are also hardened to failure and take it in their stride, making them more innovative and better trouble-shooters than your play-it-safe; always-score 100%; stick-to-what-I-know kind of students. Having worked in an organisation which promotes this ideology, I have picked up some practical strategies for creating a self-directed learning environment which are discussed in the second section of this book. Facilitating excellent learning is all about focussing on *purpose* during the time set aside for it. As you shall see in Principle Four entitled: *Inhabit Real Time*, when you focus deeply on the task at hand and complete it well, time will open up for you. In fact time will appear to stand still, allowing your full energy to be dedicated to the task at hand.

Priority Three: Marking

Have you ever loaded your car full of books on Friday afternoon only to bring them back un-touched on Monday morning? This is a familiar scenario for many teachers. The books need to be marked and despite attempting to keep on top of the job throughout the week, you have amounted a pile bigger than you can carry. You have stacked them into a plastic container (or two) or perhaps an excessively large bag-for-life and sought the assistance of two older pupils or the care-taker and put them into your car. The suspension nearly gives way at the weight of the load and you don't know how you will find the energy to unload the car again at the other end, let alone complete the task of marking the books before Monday. Throughout my career, I have actually found myself wishing for a day off work, simply so I could 'catch up' with my marking. Which, if you think of it, is a ludicrous idea: I needed a break from my job, so I could catch up with my work.

The average teacher will teach 5-6 periods a day, five days a week. Arguably, there is an exception of two and a half periods but for many, whilst these are taught by someone else, they still become your responsibility to mark. Teachers will often teach 30 pupils per lesson, which equals around 750 books per week. Even if you spend just three minutes per book, it amounts to 37.5 hours (an average work week in the UK) - just to mark books to a minimal standard. This number increases of course because each time you take a break from marking, you need to get back in your stride, which takes time, and often it is done at the end of an exhausting day or week and everything can take up to twice as long. In the next principle, we will discuss how time periods of equal length can vary in value and how using this to your advantage will enable you to multiply your productivity. You will also find useful tips to support you with marking in Principle Seven: *Batch your tasks*.

The thing about marking is that, if done properly, it is where you have the most impact as a teacher. Ironically, it is the most commonly neglected component of the three thirds of teaching. Think about it. How do you learn? You learn from your mistakes of course. If there's no audience for your work, no one to scrutinise what you have done, not only do you not know if you've done it correctly, you simply don't *care*. It is interesting that this is the most common excuse I have heard teachers make for not doing marking - the children don't read it anyway. That is precisely the point: marking is a dialogue - a professional discussion between student and teacher. When I speak, I *expect* people to listen. Similarly, when I write, I *expect* people to read it. Both you and your pupils should have an equal sense of self-respect. I take pride when I receive an indignant complaint from a pupil proclaiming that I did not mark their last piece of work. It means they have come to expect me to mark their work promptly and that they have made an effort; they are keen to find out what I made of it. Moreover, mistakes that are left unchecked become more deeply ingrained the longer they are left. You have heard of the saying 'practice makes perfect', but if what is being practised is incorrect, the student is developing to perfection something which is wrong. If you feel that marking is a part of your job you have been neglecting, I suggest you seriously consider shifting your focus away from planning and teaching and on to marking for a while. You may be surprised at the effects. As teachers we spend too much of our time planning and teaching material the pupils already know. If we just began by setting them the task and gave them feedback and a chance to resubmit, I firmly hold that they would make quicker, more lasting progress than if we spent hours planning and teaching but neglected to mark the work.

There are many tasks presented to you in your work as priorities. However, your overarching purpose should always be to facilitate learning and a focus on this will help you establish the three good habits that help you to get this done each day, namely: planning, teaching and feedback.

PRINCIPLE FOUR

INHABIT *REAL* TIME

'Time is not the main thing-it is the only thing.'

-   Miles Davis

Time is the great leveller. Everyone, whatever his circumstances has the same 24 hours in a day. So why do some people achieve so much and others so little in the same space of time? Because time is not as simple as it first appears. You need to learn how it operates and the elusions it throws up if you have any hope of working with it successfully. When you dig down, you come across some counter-intuitive but fascinating realities.

If you are to successfully dedicate your time to the priorities outlined in the previous chapter, there is a principle you need first to understand: there are two types of time. The type of time we are usually referring to when we schedule appointments and discuss timetabling is 'clock time'. The type of time that flies when we are having fun (or stands still when we are bored) can be aptly referred to as *real time*. People from certain cultures like those of the UK or US tend to focus very much on clock-time. They need to give (albeit arbitrary) units to this valuable commodity by breaking it down into sacrosanct sections on a calendar and marching around proclaiming "time is money". They read books like the very one you are reading now, take immense pleasure from being punctual and view time in a linear way, with the past behind and future in front. This idea is born from a perception of time trundling a long steadily on a track: past-present-future.

However, we must remember before we get annoyed with our colleague who arrives for a meeting half an hour late and acts like we're the one with the problem that this understanding of time is a cultural perception: it is not reality. If time perception is culturally relative, let us think about things from a different angle. For example, your colleague may perceive the (shock, horror) actual *content* of the meeting to be more important than the time it began or ends. Should you be mid-flow in conversation -about to reach a decision and then you look at your watch and announce," I'm sorry I've got another appointment," your college is likely to look at you in confusion - even if it was him who caused the meeting to start late. This is because to your colleague, you are missing the point. For him time is just an arbitrary yardstick. How could it possibly be more important than the actual events taking place? We must all be familiar with the German stereotype: buses running on time, towels on the sunbeds at 6 am and zero tolerance for late-comers. Whether or not this is actually the case is beside the point, the stereotype is supposed to represent the extreme - our cultural way of viewing clock time as of having intrinsic value over and above the purpose which we use it for. Interestingly, money has befallen a similar fate in our culture, moving from a tool to being seen as an end in itself. Other cultures tend to be stereotyped in the other direction, caring little for clock time and using it merely as an estimate if it is given at all. In some cultures, time is not seen in this linear way but it's actually viewed as moving backwards in a sense with the past opening out in front of us as revealed and true in the future behind our heads (where we have no eyes). It can be quite a liberating experience to try to refocus our attention on what can be done with the time rather than the unit with which we measure it. New possibilities are opened up when the artificial barriers are broken down. This chapter is not about the 'correct' way to view time, but how teachers can learn to perceive it in a different way so as to have a more productive relationship with it.

Whereas clock time is regular and unbiased, *real* time has a powerful present-bias. We can say we will do anything we like in the future and setting goals is important, but you cannot escape the fact that the only thing that matters and will ever matter, is now. If it isn't happening now, then it isn't part of your future. What are you doing *now*? There are literally only three possible answers to this question: thinking, conversing or doing. If you have a bias for the latter, you are likely to be more productive. This all seems logically viable, but unfortunately we tend to apply clock time to goal-setting and this causes us to take an overly simplistic view of the future, seeing it as separate and independent of today. We are all wonderful people in the future. A person may be overweight, greedy, broke and lazy in the present, yet in the future they intend to lose weight, give money to charity, save and work hard. The person relying on 'clock time' fails to see or address the significance of the self-perpetuating thoughts, feelings and circumstances which exist now; not realising that it is only what is done *today* which will cause the future to look any different. Instead, they see possible events with their current thoughts and feelings edited out, as though these will not be perpetuated beyond the present.

Real time is not about minutes and hours, but energy and focus. If you were to diarise how much work you completed at different times of the day, you will notice that you are significantly more productive at completing certain types of task at some times than others. For example, many people find that they complete far more planning at home than in the same amount of PPA time during the school day. There are a number of factors involved in this, such as the level of interruptions and levels of mental energy but it all boils down to the level of focus you are able to give to the task at hand at that particular moment. Or to put it another way, how *present* you are when you complete the task. Most of the tasks we complete only receive a fraction of our energy at any given moment, and therefore it is no wonder they take far longer to complete and require us to return to them more, either because we can't remember certain aspects of them or to correct mistakes. Another problem with not being fully focussed is that we don't complete the task in the most efficient way possible because we do not allow the creative mind space to look at the bigger picture. The key to utilising *real* time to its full capacity is in harnessing the power of *flow*.

It is very likely that you have experienced this heightened state of focus at least once before. However, it tends to be accidental and very rare so the benefits of it are not widely recognised. This is evident in the way we set up our working areas and working practices. The fifty minute lesson and the uniformity in work spaces almost seems to be set up to disrupt flow and therefore discourage the creativity in thought that comes as a result. Once the flow has been broken, momentum can take a significant amount of time to re-establish so whilst it may not always be possible to work in this state, you would ideally want to consider it the normal way of working. When you are in the state of flow, your thoughts appear as complete strings of thought, connected neatly to other ideas in all the right places. It's as though you are discovering them rather than putting them together as you go. Once you get going, you are able to use the power of momentum to bust through minor interruptions as though they don't exist and major ones even appear as obstacles to be side-stepped. You are literally blind-sighted by your ideas which seem to reveal themselves to you as fully formed objects, in such a way that it can be difficult for your 'normal' day-to-day mind to keep up with them. To break the flow would require something else to steal your focus. Your attention would need to be ripped from the object and placed somewhere else by another source, as though someone has removed a virtual reality mask mid-game. Thankfully, the idea can be dull in itself, yet it will hold your attention like a drug once you are in the flow state. In a state of flow, you are inhabiting real time. You can get anything done in real time! It simply doesn't exist in clock time and the two can't coexist either.

Those who say they have no time to (fill in the blank) should spend 10 minutes of real time on this task and see how much they can accomplish. Think about the duration of doctors' appointments! People who inhabit real time as a matter of habit understand the potential of a mere ten minutes and will never say, "I have no time to teach the children that/ mark those books/ listen to them read/ plan that enrichment activity". If you meditate, you will understand the reason for this power more deeply. The reason it is so powerful is because it is in the *present*. When you focus deeply on the task at hand and complete it well, time will open up for you. The state is characterised by intense concentration; a merging of action and awareness; a sense of control; enjoyment and most intriguingly: a distorted sense of time. Finding your flow is about finding your place in real time, where you experience abundance in time. The concept is particularly poignant in the context of teaching because it is especially elusive. We tend to assume that pupils will behave in such a way that you will not be allowed to focus. However this comes from the belief that pupils require your attention to overcome barriers in their learning. You will find that if you respect *your* flow, you will be helping them to find their own. You will naturally end up doing this in small ways, for example, instead of rewarding pupils for working in silence, you will simply say, "Do you mind speaking a little more quietly? I am finding it difficult to concentrate." I have never had a negative response to this request. In my experience, students tend to respond with surprise, apology and/or intrigue. They almost always put their heads down and assume a focussed state. Long periods of unrequested silence often ensue and the students may even astound themselves with their output. When your students have discovered flow for themselves, you may find yourself apologising for interrupting them to tell them that it is break time, so powerful is the state that has gripped them. Research has found flow to be linked to intrinsic motivation and autonomy and plenty has been written about facilitating this state in educational contexts. John Hopkins used *functional magnetic resource imaging* to look at the brain waves of jazz musicians in flow and found that the state was associated with transient hypo-frontality. In layman's terms this means that the part of the brain responsible for self-doubt is shut down, and pleasure-inducing chemicals like serotonin are released which also increase ability to solve problems. The state is very close to the brain's alpha or 'day dreaming' mode which means you have that characteristic single-mindedness and numbness to distractions.

I would go as far as to suggest it would just be akin to the natural way our brains are programmed to work at the creative level and that our fascination with clock-time has entailed that we rarely use our brains to their full capacity. Luckily, there are many practical ways to deliberately cultivate the flow state upon command, meaning that the transition from clock to real time can be made when required. First, we must:

Get into the Right Mind Space

You will need to ensure your mind is in the right place to focus. You may choose to put on some calming music or sound waves designed for focus. I often find that in guiding students to find their flow, adding music after a few minutes working in silence works best. I always ask students if they wouldn't mind before I play music as this shows respect for their own precious focus time.

Make Sure you are Prepared

Whilst I advise using music - especially the use of headphones, I would advise against an overreliance on 'comforters'. I often work with people who cannot focus unless they have their favourite pen, cold water, a selection of snacks, have been to the toilet etc. Such fussiness not only eats into time but it also limits the times and places during which work can be completed. I would recommend always carrying a pen for marking, a sharp pencil (with a rubber at the end), your diary and a notebook. A light laptop (and the means to charge it) provide useful but non-essential additions to this set. Once you are practiced, the external environment will matter very little to you and you can achieve flow with only the simplest of instruments to capture your ideas.

Set a Timer

Before you start a task, decide how long you will allocate to it and set a timer. You may not realise it but you will lose a significant amount of time looking at your watch or clock and then refocussing each time you return to your task. There is also a certain amount of time involved in processing the time and thinking about implications. Recognise this as clock time interfering with real time. Remember the two are unable to coexist. Be realistic about how much of the task you expect to complete in the allocated time. Principle Five entitled *stick to your timetable* will help you consider this in advance so it will not take up essential mind-space. There are lots of different theories about how much time you should be able to focus in one session. One school of thought says we work best in a pulse and pause routine rather than in solid, unbroken blocks of time. The exact length of the pulses and pauses tends to vary wildly amongst writers on this subject. A popular routine is the 'Pomodoro' technique which argues that 25 minutes work, followed by a five minute break is the average optimal time for focus. In case you were wondering, it's called the Pomodoro Technique because the person who invented it used a tomato kitchen timer. However, 25 minutes is only loosely based on an average focus time. Some find it too short and others too long. I would argue that if such a rhythm exists, then you should find your own one.

The reason you decide on a set time is that it's a commitment to yourself. If you don't set a time it's like kicking a ball without looking at the goal. We could argue about how arbitrary the target is all day long but no target will mean no accomplishment in the end. You have to be intentional in order to focus. I would suggest that no length of time is too short which do accomplish something meaningful, especially if you get used to harnessing the power of flow. At the other end of the spectrum, if you do work for too long after you begin to find it difficult to focus, you will be spending more energy than necessary to accomplish the required outcome and would do better to return to the task after a short break.

Work Until the Timer Stops You

Now you know it will be just you and the task for however long, you had better make the best of it and get to grips with it! If it really is pointless like your brain keeps telling you, then just get it out of the way. When you work in this way, you will usually find you get to a place where you could keep on going forever - flow. The more you practice this type of uninterrupted working, the quicker it takes you to get into this state. You will begin to feel as though the timer will never go off but trust that it will.

When it does, you will feel as though you feel when an alarm breaks a deep slumber: you really wish it hadn't. This will happen regardless of whether or not you were looking forward to the task to begin with. Such is the power of flow.

Do Regular Mind Clearance

Using a capturing system as described in principle one is crucial as it cuts out the cerebral noise and clutter so you can immerse yourself in deep work. All of us are in the habit of using our mind space (particularly the short-term memory) as an in-tray to store the many incomplete ideas we have on a daily basis. Even if you have successfully implemented the advice in Principle Two, you will still find residual clutter gets dumped there without your noticing. This clutter has an irritating habit of making itself known as soon as you quiet your mind. Mind clearance is the act of clearing the clutter out, capturing it and putting it into your system. Energy varies throughout tasks and different stages will take different amounts of time to complete. Due to the law of inertia, getting started on a task can take the bulk of the total energy required to complete it from start to finish. If you have ever push-started a car or switched on a mobile phone when it is low on battery you will understand what I mean. This makes getting started the most important part, even if you do this and then leave it alone for a short while. If you don't leave it too long, the task will still be rolling when you return to it and it will be so much easier to begin again.

Flow will happen on its own if all the conditions are right, but if you wait for these conditions to coexist spontaneously whilst going about your life as most of us do, you may only experience this state a few times in your life. But the state makes you happier, more confident and more productive, so it will become a powerful ally to even the busiest of individuals if they can cultivate it intentionally and conjure it up as often as possible. If you can achieve this for yourself, you can do so for your students. In order to cultivate as much flow time as possible, clock time will be your ally. However, you will need to plan your flow minutes using clock-time beforehand. The minimum I would recommend is twenty-five minutes (one Pomodoro) per day. This may not seem like significant amount but real time is worth many times more than the twenty-five units of clock time. The Law of incremental gains tells us that a small, regular amount of practise each day is worth far more than the same amount of time in a more sporadic block. This is due to a number of factors including the time spent having to refocus between blocks and the loss of opportunities to engage with the task in between the flow state as it leaves the forefront of your mind.

Once you have scheduled your flow time, you will need to train yourself to protect the time. Having a smaller amount will make it easier for you to do this psychologically but it is surprising how easy it can be to allow the menial tasks to run over into it. This is why you need to teach your mind to crave the flow time! Luckily, this is not as difficult to achieve as it sounds as the flow-state is not only efficient but it can be addictive. If you have established a healthy habit of completing your tasks (as outlined in Principle One), you may notice the Zeigarnik effect appears stronger. This is because tasks requiring the flow state often take longer to complete than basic tasks, you may find they play on your mind, inviting you to come back and work on them. You can use this to your advantage, causing your pupils (and you) to gain extra traction towards your desired goals. All you have to do is schedule the flow time each day for a set time and start and end when you said you would.

With what you know about the value of real time in mind, you are ready to use planning to make the most of

81

what is available to you.

PRINCIPLE FIVE

PLAN SMART

'A goal without a plan is just a wish.'

- Antoine De Saint-Exupery

Planning, preparation and assessment time: This sacred non-contact time was given to us lowly teachers following a drawn out fight and now sits as a slot on our timetable. We protect the precious few minutes we are allowed each week away from the daily demands of teaching. Yet we rarely use the time for the allotted purpose. Interruptions seem the most obvious culprit in this situation. But are interruptions really to blame or are we just making the choice to be distracted? Whilst time has been allocated time to the task at hand, this in itself is not enough to compete the job. The irony is we need to actually plan our planning, preparation and assessment time so that the choice to be distracted no longer exists. Scheduling allows planning to take place in the same way as getting your diet right will allow your exercise to have the desired effect.

Planning is an intangible concept. Without wishing to get deeply philosophical, it is important that we are on 'the same page' when it comes to discuss what is meant by planning. Whilst we teachers in particular frequently perceive it as a paper or digital map of our future actions (usually taught lessons), it is something aside from this. Planning occurs all the time without our awareness but when it is done consciously, is one of the most powerful forces a person can behold. Think of planning as an algorithm which is set in motion before an action takes place. It takes place even before we are aware of it but it necessarily precedes each action. There is scientific debate as to whether it occurs even prior to the 'idea' stage and some very compelling evidence that this is in fact the case, but for the sake of this book, let's call planning the next step after the formation of an idea which might lead to it coming to fruition. When you plan, you are intending for a future action to take place at a given future time.

In theory, you can teach very well without 'planning' in the traditional sense. I recommend you take a spin on the supply circuit if you have any doubt as to this fact. It is, however, an exhausting (and therefore unsustainable practice) which requires you to think in both the short and medium term planning stage at once. Whether you plan months or moments ahead, the planning will still always take place prior to the teaching. There is no such thing as planning not done. It is simply a case of how far ahead the planning is done. If you leave it to moments ahead, you cannot spend excessive time on the process. This is possibly a very good thing, until you realise there is a finite amount of time you need to spend on planning to execute an adequate lesson. Once you tip the balance and spend less time than you need to, you are potentially losing time to mistakes within the lesson itself. According to clock time, two minutes spent at the photocopier is the same two minutes whether it be the week before the lesson, right before the lesson or during the lesson. However, in real time, completing the task during or right before the lesson will impair the flow of the lesson and possibly the behaviour of the pupils. On the flip-side, plan too far ahead and you will lose time. For example, if you try to get your photocopying in too early, your attention may be spent trying to recall whether or not you did it, attempting to locate it and even in redoing it unnecessarily. If your long term planning is secure, then last minute planning can be completed much more easily and will have greater impact because you will have the long-term goals in mind.

Each teacher will have a unique amount of time they will need to spend planning their lessons to avoid potential time costs. I would recommend experimenting with this number. Remain as close as you can to the minimum amount of time you need to spend planning as this will help you find the correct balance and will ultimately reduce the amount of time you need to complete it.

In theory, even if you were to throw your planning document in the recycling bin immediately after having completed it, it would still have been time well-spent. The very act of planning is powerful because it forces you to think about outcomes and to project them into the future. This is in fact the strength that defines us as a species. Planning is the only way to address problems before they arise and to see the intricate ways in which knowledge and skills can be connected: one of the many reasons it saves you time in the long term. As the product of real planning, learning is deeper and more meaningful because of the way it is interconnected with other aspects of the curriculum and delivered in line with the pupils' development. Without true planning, the learning is likely to be less personalised to the needs of the student and as a result, you may need to cover the material over and over again. The type of planning referred to above as 'true planning' needs to be differentiated from what is typically understood to be planning. The type of planning you leave for a supply teacher is inherently instructional. If you plan in this manner as a matter of course, it can cause you to spend more time than necessary and may tempt you to try to micro-manage the lesson to ensure it is carried out exactly as intended, attempting to problems in advance of them actually occurring. If there is one greater waste of time than spending time worrying about what might happen, it is spending time attempting to solve problems that have not yet happened.

It goes without saying that planning is not for only for lessons, but for life in general. It is a type of forward reflection that most disciplines have built into their fabric. Because it is generally taken for granted, we rarely think of planning as a form of reflection. As a result, we rarely utilise this dimension of planning. Your timetable or calendar give you a guide as to the activities you should be doing at any one time but if you want to make progress, it is important that you reflect on the outcomes over and above the means to achieve them. If systems are the transport by which we achieve our goals, then the outcomes are the final destination we use to set our course. When planning is perceived as a set of instructions for future action, it can lead to resentment of the act of planning. We learn that it is inevitable in the future that many of these planned actions will turn out to be less effective than we thought, downright impossible or even obsolete in light of real time circumstances. When this occurs, we abandon the 'plan' for a more intuitive approach. As a result, we come to view these aspects of the planning as wasted time.

This difficulty is dependent on how planning is perceived. Consider two types of planning: that which you do for yourself versus that which you produce for someone else to follow. The distinction will be immediately apparent if you have ever been told by a senior leader that planning should be done to such a level that anyone can follow the lesson simply by reading what you had written on your plan. In my opinion, this advice is deeply misguided, controlling and should immediately be discarded. The planning document designed for someone else is nothing short of a set of instructions, required only if placing a non-teaching member of staff in charge of the class. The planning you do for yourself is likely to exist as a set of cues and reminders. Perhaps it resides not in a document but a set of systems and routines that operate in your teaching space. Effective planning is far more than a tool to aid your memory. It is an opportunity to partake in the most valuable type of reflection - looking at the bigger picture and therefore the larger purpose of your actions. Don't let someone commend your planning based on the clarity and specificity of the instructions on your document. Any cover teacher worth their salt will need nothing more than the lesson objective to fulfil the intention of said lesson. In the absence of the objective, they should be able to take into account the circumstances and set an appropriate one of their own.

If you wish to reach a particular destination and you have become fixated not on the destination but on the method of travel, when the train breaks down you may get so frustrated that you return home and abandon the trip. Like the student who couldn't complete his or her homework because their computer broke down. Perhaps it genuinely didn't occur to them to use another method to complete the task. Perhaps it is simply an excuse. However, if you focus on the destination, barely making mention of the means of travel, when the train breaks down, you *will* find another way. There will be no mental energy fixated on the broken down train because it instantly becomes just as irrelevant as all the other unsuitable modes of transport you didn't take. If you are particularly invested in the destination, you will walk if you have to. When you view planning as the act of identifying outcomes, it leads to finality and as we have seen in Principle Two, finishing things is inherently satisfying. Planning is unavoidable. It is simply a case of how long you can put it off. If you do it too late, you end up doing so in a stressed and inefficient state but you will need to do it all the same. Once you get into the habit of planning for outcomes with only the smallest attention to the means of achieving these, you may find that planning is more enjoyable and you will be less likely to put it off.

Now we have covered what is to be understood by planning, let us discuss what this means in practical terms for the Time Management Teacher. Let's begin with the most basic and easily recognisable unit of planning: the lesson plan. As far as lesson planning goes, you are probably familiar with the rule of thumb: 'Don't reinvent the wheel'. However, teacher will understand that this is often easier said than done for two reasons:

1. It is often discouraged - every child is unique and planning, teaching and feedback needs to be distinctly tailored to individual needs and also relevant to current affairs and themed days etc.

2. It can often seem easier to draw things up from scratch, as it can be difficult to find the relevant resources/ solutions/ routines etc.: especially for an experienced teacher.

I will address these reasons one at a time.

It is often discouraged

The main reason using ready-made plans is discouraged is that they are not tailored to meet the needs of individual children. One way around this is to re-read and annotate plans, adapting them to specific children and classes. However, this can make planning difficult to follow, essentially defeating its purpose. In reality, the practise of using someone else's plans saves very little (if any) time compared with re-writing plans. This is because in planning, the majority of time and energy is expended on understanding and trouble-shooting the plans (rather than the manual aspect of writing them out). For this reason, it can be better to get into the habit of writing plans for yourself every time. The way to do this fast is rather than saving your weekly planning and re-using it each year, to use formulas for planning lessons. This means that when planning try, as often as possible, to do things in exactly the same way. The best pre-made planning template is one made by your habits. Planning by algorithm maximises your ability to copy and paste whilst keeping your planning specific to your particular cohort. Moreover, the benefits of planning in this way much outweigh the downsides. Using a formula saves writing and explanation time, gets children into good habits, frees up the mind for other considerations and can enable you to teach a range of skills in a balanced way so that children can direct their own learning.

It is easier to draw things up from scratch

I've heard this assertion numerous times yet I always think if it's that easy to draw it from scratch, you've probably done it too many times! The reason it's probably easier to create something from scratch is usually not because it is easy to complete, but because it would take so long to locate and produce a copy. This is usually the result of poor organisation. To avoid this, try to create and store things in a way that makes them easy find and duplicate. Even consider how many duplicates you will need in the near future and produce them at the outset. Use your physical or digital filing system to store master copies under a logical key word and when locating resources, stay organised. You should have a digital filing system set up already in which to save files for planning and I would recommend limiting your levels of filing to prevent a back log. The first layer I would recommend should have five files:

1. Planning (dated with the year)
2. Assessment (dated with the year)
3. Admin (dated with the year)
4. Old (all files not relevant to that year).
5. Personal (all files not directly relevant to teaching and learning)

Inside your planning file, you should have:

- Long Term Planning: containing all the files relating to the broad overview of the year.
- Medium Term Planning: If you teach more than one subject, the Medium Term planning layer should have a separate file for each subject you teach. If not, the next layer should be one for each class/ year group you teach (obviously this may not be necessary if you only teach one year group). The final layer should be split into terms and half terms. I recommend terms rather than other units because it relates specifically to the days in that year. The specific details, should be tailored to whatever is easiest to use. These categories will provide a useful starting point.

Long-Term Planning

Long-Term Planning should be very quick and simple to create. This is the most important layer of planning as it requires a brain process which is unique to viewing the bigger picture. However, it is the easiest layer to neglect. If you don't produce a long-term plan, you won't get the benefit of this bigger-picture planning. Yet short and medium term planning will happen whether you make time for them or not. Looking at things from above like this allows you to pinpoint the essential components of learning and to track these over time. Short and medium term planning can get you bogged down with immediate and often less-significant concerns and this can mean you lose sight of your priorities. The long term plan gives you an idea of the topics to be covered at a glance. This is mainly so you can ensure you cover all the necessary objectives during the time available. This might be the full course of an academic year, but it is more efficient if it covers the length of the time frame leading up to each summative assessment. It is helpful to calculate the amount of time available for the assessment cycle in days or lessons so that coverage of topic areas is realistically placed. Generally speaking, if you can, it is much better to produce such a plan without any special resources. This will enable you to remain focussed on the outcome you want to achieve without getting bogged down with too much detail. All it requires is the broad spectrum overview of what you will be teaching at any given time throughout the academic year. When long-term planning, ensure that you keep in mind your purpose: to facilitate learning. Will the children make demonstrable progress during the period for which you are planning? What will this look like?

Medium-Term Planning

Medium-term planning is to the long term plan as the diary is to the timetable. Your long term plan is your broad strokes overview of planning and the medium term breaks it down according to the feasibility of each day. Prior to resource collection, it is ideal to have this type of plan completed as it will save you time planning for lessons that won't realistically happen. It won't take long and requires the use of your calendar and timetable.

1. First create a grid with a row for each lesson you will teach during a typical week (use your timetable to inform this) and a column for each stage of the lesson plus resources and homework.

2. Put into the grid any routines you repeat during each of the lessons on a typical week. E.g. a spelling test to begin each spelling lesson, or a quiz to end each history lesson. If you teach the same class the same subject more than once per week, I would recommend theming the days e.g.

always teach a particular aspect of the subject on a particular day. The theme could be a skill or subject area, as this will save you hours of thinking time working out what to cover.

3. Copy and paste the grid containing all the required information for as many weeks in the unit (or half term) depending on how your teaching and summative assessment cycle works.

4. Using your calendar, fill in the dates for each week (one table represents on week) and also label them using a fraction format (e.g. week 2 of 6).

5. Next, use your calendar to fill in all bank holidays, school holidays, INSET days, parents' evenings, extra-curricular events and theme days such as international women's day and the like. You will be surprised how much seemingly unrelated events will affect your ability to teach a 'normal' syllabus, as they will affect staffing, resource availability, the students' and even your ability to focus! These are really helpful as they will save you planning a regular syllabus when it is not necessary.

6. Now you are ready to count up all the available days for teaching the required syllabus up until the point of assessment. Try not to panic but be prepared for this number to be far less than you were expecting!

7. Now look at your long-term plan. Ask what do my students absolutely need to know prior to the end of this cycle? Again, a seasoned teacher will be able to write this list of outcomes off the top of

their heads, using the long-term plan as a trigger. You will be left with a specific amount of days (from step 6) to address this list of outcomes.

8. Finally it is time to pencil this list into the empty spaces on the grid as you see fit. Use the homework column and theme days for creative consolidation where you think it might be required. Otherwise, leave them blank and formative assessment will tell you what the students need to work more on.

Short-Term Planning

It is important not to complete short-term planning further than one assessment cycle in advance or it could end up wasting more time than it saves. Whilst this is the detailed stage, it needn't be time consuming. Here are the stages of short term planning:

1. You will use the shell created during the Medium-Term planning stage to prepare your short term planning. I recommend going through the resource-collection phase prior to this stage as the availability of resources will likely have a significant impact on the specifics of your daily planning.

2. Refer to the resources you have collected and plan out your lessons. If you teach more than one subject, always plan one subject at a time, so that you can get in the correct mind-set and into your flow. I would recommend adding simple 'steps for success' instructions to complete the tasks at this stage, as it is much easier to think of them at this stage then trying to conceive them at the start of a lesson. They also save explanation time

during lessons and mean that the lesson can begin immediately for those students who use initiative, because they can be displayed on the board at the very start of the lesson. Keep filling in your lessons until you reach the end of the assessment cycle. This is useful even if you teach one subject as you can work on one series of lessons at a time. E.g. all research-based lessons and then all writing-based lessons.

3. Once you have planned all the lessons, you can begin preparing resources in advance. If you have an assistant who can use initiative, simply give them access to your plans and files. They will learn how many copies to make and how to present them. Alternatively, prepare a single copy of all the resources you will need and put it into a folder marked with the week number on it. I have folders marked 1-7 which I refresh each half term. If each item is to be copied the same amount of times, a single post-it will do for the lot. If not post-it certain papers individually and put a post-it on the folder for the rest. If you use digital presentations in your lessons, prepare these in advance. By doing a whole day or even week in one presentation, you can save time setting up for each lesson. I usually just put in the dates and learning objectives, and then add the instructions for any tasks as copied and pasted directly from my plan.

Using Presentations

There are a number of benefit to using an electronic presentation. It relieves the brain of the burden of judging the sequential aspect of the lesson, leaving it to focus on the content, it is immediately engaging to have a visual prompt and it can be referred back to at any time to revisit the content of the lesson. Usually thought of as a teaching aid, presentations can be used as a planning tool in their own right. Certainly if you are in the habit of using presentations, you may find it unnecessary to complete any other type of plan.

Using internet planning resources

Internet resources can be really useful at times, but it's important to remember the reason we use them is to save time and paper. However, if our usage is not strategic, such resources can become the biggest time and paper wasters of all. Because of the way they are organised and means by which we access them, resource websites can become black holes and consume PPA time with very little to show as outcomes. The resources are located on the internet. Whenever we go on the internet, we can easily get caught up in minutia and before we know it, we become tangled in the big World Wide Web with little grasp of what we were looking for to begin with. Computers are home to our calendars, email systems and various other media just waiting to steal our attention and they are prone to technical glitches. Never go in unarmed. Prior to using a search engine, identify specifically what you want to obtain and have a clear idea of when and how you will use it. Unless you can give the resource a specific day and time during which you intend to use it - don't go there: chances are it will never get used. If you find digital resources from websites such as *Twinkl*, make sure you block time to do so systematically. Before you enter the search, identify what you are looking for and a suitable alternative if this is not available. No unnecessary consideration should take place when you are in the website or your mind will wander and that's how you get lost in a black hole. Your mind-set should be purely fixed on retrieval. Get in. Get out.

It helps to have your planning completed to the medium term phase before you begin. The medium term planning document outlines your focus for the term or unit. Focusing on one subject at a time, download anything that is relevant to that learning principle (try not to look in detail at the resources as you go as this will waste valuable time and is likely to take you off on a tangent). Remember, you can think about how to put the resources together once you get to the short term planning stage. But this should not be your concern during the collection phase. If you work from your plan and download the resources you will need for each lesson you have scheduled, you have automatically identified a day and time for each resource. If you teach more than one subject, make sure you focus on one subject at a time. Even within a single subject, you can batch the domains of that subject area. If you already have an appropriate calendar scheduled out, you can quickly collect resources to the end of the school year, as this will be comprised of a surprisingly small number of days when you skip out the holidays, INSET days and assessment days. As a bonus, it will save you time when you want to locate your plans another time, especially when you are looking a year or more later.

Using Dictation

Dictation can be used as a practical way to speed up your planning. It works because it enables you to sail on the power of flow by just talking about what you will do for each stage and that voice being converted into an immediate digital record. Unfortunately, the software is still at a rather crude stage of its development. However, if you can hone this skill now, you will be ahead of the curve in this regard. Speaking rather than typing is the way forward. I find that using Microsoft Word on my iPhone is the most effective way to use dictation as a software is built into the iPhone. The finished document can be saved on OneDrive or email to yourself and this is the fastest way I've ever been able to do plans. It also has the benefit of helping you to plan much more intuitive lessons which make sense when you hear them back whilst walking the dog.

Stick to *Your* Timetable

If you don't plan your time, someone else will plan for you. Just as planning is the blueprint for your lessons, your timetable is the blueprint for your day. You wouldn't dream of beginning a construction project without planning first, or attempting a journey without using a map. However, strangely, many people go about their day making on the spot decisions about what they should be doing and when. Therefore, it is not surprising that so few people use their time effectively. The timetable is the vehicle whereby teachers are given clear direction as to the exact amount of time they are expected to spend teaching. You are expected to spend ninety percent of lesson time teaching and ten percent planning and marking. Having distinct slots on a timetable called 'lessons' is a system which has been established to ensure this takes place. This may sound obvious, but that is only because the idea has worked so well for so long we no longer question it; if you really think about it, the concept of lessons is ingenious. The best other professions could do to micromanage their workers is draft in as many meetings and deadlines as they reasonably could. Teachers effectively have between 5 and 8 'meetings' scheduled every day (this is without additional meetings). In theory, it follows that teachers should be particularly efficient, as a means scheduling each working minute is built right in to their job description. However, whilst this to some extent true, there are a few pretty significant problems with the arrangement. Firstly, because it comes with the job, teachers will - at best - take the timetable for granted. At worst, they will see abiding by it as a chore. If you work in an organisation with a centralised timetable, you may feel that it restricts your professional independence. We have learnt to be compliant and to follow the rules from the earliest of ages and the teaching timetable exploits this tendency to the extreme; I even know some teachers who reduce the amount they drink to prevent the interruption of unscheduled breaks. Even in those increasingly rare organisations where the teacher is allowed to create a timetable for themselves, they will be restricted by considerations such as a standardised template, the amount of hours they are expected to spend teaching a particular subject, or the availability of staff or resources. Furthermore, it is likely that the timetable will need to be revised regularly causing the process to become laborious.

Secondly, you don't need to be a maths teacher to work out that the balance offered to you doesn't give appropriate weight to planning and marking. This is no accident. Due to its complexity, organisation of the teaching timetable is often dictated by an external source. Often the overseer to whom the timetable is outsourced is sufficiently removed from the 'frontline' to become almost entirely reliant on the use of abstract data to assess its performance. Judgements pertaining to timetabling are likely to be driven by a focus on raising certain measures such as attainment whilst minimising others such as expenditure. Schools, as with all organisations, exist to produce certain outcomes outside of themselves: they exist to produce results for students. They do not exist for teachers. It is your job to exist for yourself. Otherwise *you* will cease to exist except as part of the system.

However useful and proficient the timetable you use, the fact is: if you follow it unquestioningly, someone else's priorities will dictate how you spend your time. As your job title dictates, you are a *teacher*. Therefore, if you are being employed in this role, you are expected to spend the large majority of your time doing as your role suggests -*and actively teaching*. Make no apologies. This is your job. On top of this, the large majority of teachers also double up as a child-care solution for young people who are not to be left unsupervised. So when you are not timetabled to teach, someone else is being paid to do so, or at the very least to fulfil a supervisory capacity for which you are also being paid.

A teaching timetable is a way of ensuring you are being deployed effectively and that your employer is getting the best possible value for money. You are expected to plan and mark to a high standard; in fact you *need* to do so in order to teach effectively. The catch is: if you don't manage it within the given 2.5 hours of planning and preparation time - that is *your* problem. You have no choice but to do so in your own time. But timetabling, if you own it, can be far more than it first appears. The act of assigning specific future actions and goals to a specific time and space can be an enlightening and powerful capacity. If you want to achieve any goal in life, you don't need much more than the ability to schedule and to stick to that schedule to turn your life around. Human actions result either from impulse (such as flinching at a loud noise) or from *ideas* (such as filling in a job application form). Actions of the first type are significant but should, in modern times, be rare. However, even those conscious actions resulting directly from ideas will often become close to impulse or 'autopilot' actions. This happens when we do them repeatedly enough to form a habit. Then the action resulting from that original idea becomes impulse, and we tend to lose sight of the purpose behind it – but do it anyway. Ideas, as Kim Perell explains in 'The Execution Factor' are 'a dime a dozen'. And not all of them are good. I'm sure you have taken an action and asked yourself 'why am I doing this?' If you have, you most likely remember it as a moment which had a profound effect on your life. I have had many such experiences and remember each as a turning point. The reason we have these moments, is because the idea upon which our repeated actions were based has expired to such a degree that it belongs to a completely different paradigm from the one you are currently inhabiting. The jarring impact is so powerful that it forces you awake, as if from a dream. The lowly timetable harnesses the effect of this principle, allowing us to reflect on the ideas behind all our planned actions and enabling us to keep in touch with why we are doing them in real time.

There is no more to successfully achieving a goal than the series of actions which lead to it. Notice I said actions, rather than ideas. The goal is the idea but it is static and fleeting. It is the next step that counts. The action. And where do actions occur? Actions occur in time and space. If you do not assign desired actions to a given time and place, either in advance or moments before, they will probably never materialise. They will remain an idea, lingering like a cloud of smoke for long enough to reassure you that you won't forget it; then before you know it: it is gone. As I mentioned earlier, the only actions which will occur without pre-assignment to given a time and space are those which are habitual. You need to believe that it is true before you can see that it is true. Hence why so many don't bother. Your first step is to make the action of assigning a time and place to every intended action. I mean every action. You need to assign mundane actions like buying pet food to a specific time and place just as you would schedule a trip to Thailand. At first it will be a deliberate effort. You will have to consciously ask yourself: *when will I do this? Where will I do this?* And it will be hard because you aren't used to it. You may naturally conclude that you couldn't possibly do this for every action. The first time you try, you will probably hear a subconscious voice in the distance saying that you don't need to. The voice will try to convince you that you will remember to do this or that and that you don't need to schedule such a small thing. If you are particularly well-versed in negative self-talk, the voice may even go so far as to ridicule you. You can characterise this voice as your 'future self'. The future-self is the part of you who will sabotage you by not bothering to get out of bed at the time you said you would or choosing not to go to the gym at the last minute. This same self is not only lazy and manipulative but it is also downright forgetful and preoccupied with other things. We all have these future selves, but oddly and perhaps naively, we really over-estimate their capabilities. Some go as far as to assume our future-selves are *better* than us. These are the people who put off until tomorrow what can be done today. Sometimes indefinitely. The good news is that if we frequently ask *when?* And *where?* Regarding every action, it will become a natural and effortless part of the decision making process. Using an electronic calendar is a useful prompt, as when you enter an event, it always asks you to enter the time, duration and location. Thankfully, a technique known as 'time-boxing' can make this a much easier process. Time-boxing involves allocating set periods on your long-term schedules to a specific type of action. It can help if these are regular slots, such as always assigning Monday afternoons to marking. PPA slots should always have a theme, such as assessment or planning with remaining time allocated to any other responsibilities to ensure that a proportionate amount of time is spent on each. This means, when it comes to assigning a particular time to a particular action, there should already be a protected timeslot in which it should fit neatly: *a place for everything and everything in its place.*

This thoughtful forward planning allows you to consider potential clashes and other problems which will save you time later. Most importantly though, it gives you the chance to consider whether actions are the best use of your time: i.e. that they are in line with your purpose. You may think that you only plan what you will do with your time on a timetable, and that the rest of the time you inhabit a planning free existence. However, you should remember such a realm does not exist, however impulsive or 'laid back' we think we are, as was discussed earlier, in reality you are *always* planning your time – even if it is merely moments in advance.

Moreover, every action we take is a decision *not* to do something else, meaning that if we don't *forward* plan, we lack the overview to make the best possible decision for the future, and end up always choosing the best possible decision for right now. This means we have not added any benefit to our future selves and sadly any good ideas never become reality - they are fleeting and often recurring moments of insight that constitute the first step into creating something new. If they are not scheduled, the second step will never occur because by default, they are concerned with the future and not with the now. Thankfully, you don't need to wait for good ideas: if you provide the right frame of mind, they come to you though all your senses. However, you will need to wait for them to flourish into a finished sequence of actions and that is only after you have taken the first step. What makes a good idea for a lesson? One that leads to the outcome you want to achieve. What is the best way to mark your books? Finish marking them. How do you achieve great lesson ideas and marked books? Assign them to a place and time.

I have met many people who realise the power of immediacy: doing things now. However, it is important to grasp that if you don't take the immediate option, this often means it won't get done at all. This sounds incredibly final and many people disregard this idea, convincing themselves they don't mean they will *never* do it. Just not *now*. However, if you are not living on purpose *now*, then there literally is no other time. There are only ever present 'nows' and future 'nows'. You might make a note of it on a list and this will increase your chances of remembering to complete the item. However, this action at best puts you in the same situation you were when you had the idea, forcing you to repeat the first step again. In any case, if you don't schedule a regular slot to address items on your list, you may never be in the position again to take the first step. However, this doesn't mean immediacy is the only option for task completion, and it is usually not the best option. When you complete all your tasks as soon as you get them, you live in a cycle of reactivity and this means you never get time to plan. The alternative is to spend some of the time you would have spent achieving the task planning when you will do it. At first glance, this option can appear inefficient as compared with the immediacy option. It is almost like the option of paying a small amount of interest for the benefit of paying in instalments. As a general rule, if something takes longer to capture then to complete, it should be completed right there and then. You may think that this is the same as writing it on a list but it is not; you need to assign it to a time and place. The crucial difference between simply making a note of an idea (mentally or otherwise) and scheduling it into the calendar is that the latter forces you to assign a next step to the action. It is the same thing you would need to do if you took action right there and then. Say the idea was teaching a creative English lesson in an outside area. It occurs to you whilst you are relaxed out for a walk in the autumn - most probably during the school holidays (otherwise known as 'teacher reflection time'). It seems like a great idea and you make a note of it to look at when you get back. However, when you arrive back at school, you immediately become embroiled in numerous demands on your time and attention. A parent wishing to speak you about this, some pupils about that, the Headteacher about the other. Before you know it, there is a last-minute scramble for some missing resource and an impromptu learning walk is due to take place any minute. Very quickly, your inspiring lesson idea gets downgraded from 'excellent' to 'impractical and darn-right ridiculous.' Furthermore, if the idea resurfaces, it is likely to be at an equally inconvenient time. This is more than an unhappy coincidence; it is because such ideas cannot arise unless your mind is relaxed. However, rather inconveniently, this is also the time when taking action seems least appealing or is impractical. In this way, step one: *having the idea* is repeated over and over and over again. If the idea ever does get off the ground, it will have taken far longer than necessary to execute due to the sheer amount of repetition at the earliest phase of its fruition.

To add to this, the idea loses the opportunity to gather momentum - a concept which is gravely unaccounted for in the execution of ideas. People typically grossly overestimate the time it takes to complete tasks because they are so used to this extended period whereby an idea is conceptualised repeatedly without any further action being taken. The best way to prevent the loss of momentum when you are forced to stop a task before it is completed is to identify the next action and to specify when the action will take place. This way, you have already considered the potential barriers to that action taking place and you have given a purpose to that future moment in time, so that precious time will not be wasted in deciding what to do.

Of course you managed to achieve many things in your life thus far without timetabling them. You are a teacher aren't you? This proves that progress is possible without scheduling. However, the timetable gives you the power to become much more efficient and effortless with the progress you make. It enables you to step back, look at the bigger picture and specify the exact most meaningful use of your time at any given moment when you could be doing an infinite number of things. This becomes clearer when we examine what shapes our behaviour when we live off timetable. Our actions tend to occur according to the following criterion: Habitual actions; actions we know will feel good; and urgent and pressing actions.

This helps us to see why so many long term ideals remain undone and why schools need timetables. The use of the subjunctive mood and other obscure grammatical concepts are neither urgent nor enjoyable for the majority of pupils (or teachers for that matter) who nonetheless work diligently for several hours per week on the path to mastering them. The timetable is the ultimate instrument of control; yet we rarely use it to take control of our own lives. Sadly, most of the time boxing has been done for us, by someone else. Each day you are given 1020 waking minutes (less if you sleep more than seven hours per night). Your employer will jealously guard 360 of those minutes and it is your job to protect the rest. If time were money, I am betting you would be much more careful with it. Imagine someone was demanding high rent from you in order for you to have somewhere to live, would you voluntarily give them more money than necessary? Would you lose track of how much you gave out on a daily basis? Surely not; yet that is what we do with our time. Think of it like this: if time and money were equal, you must pay out £360 per day from your £1020 daily budget. However, you can't earn more time. You must simply use what you have been given as efficiently as possible. Now looking at those remaining minutes should inspire you to invest the vast majority to give yourself a better future.

Interestingly, when we live *on* timetable, the non-timetable criterion rarely apply. You don't stop in the middle of the lesson you are teaching to answer the phone or do something 'fun'. When you are on timetable, other possibilities are irradiated because you are committed to the idea that what you are doing at the present moment is exactly what you *should* be doing. Even if it is teaching an otherwise irrelevant grammar concept. As we discussed, the power of the timetable resides in the fact that it forces you to define the next action. This is the crucial component here because it naturally moves the idea to the next stage along its path to fruition. When you place the next action into a future time slot, you are deciding in advance to prioritise this action which in turn forces you to trouble-shoot any consequences of choosing *this* action over its alternatives. Furthermore, defining next actions mitigates against many of the reasons why the intended actions may not occur. For example, many things don't get done because we forget about them. However, it is OK to forget the original idea when you have a next action: the idea was merely a stepping stone which can be disregarded once then next action has been formulated. Another very common reason actions fail to take place is more 'urgent' things getting in the way but identifying when you will complete the next action means that during that time, you are inaccessible. You have already decided what you will be doing with that time and the 'on-air' light is on outside. Interruptions will be assessed far more conservatively in terms of what is considered 'urgent' and following interruptions, you are more likely to get back on with the task you identified. Another excuse for not completing a task at a given time is that resources you need are not present. This is far less likely when the action is considered in advance and if it does occur, the problem is easily overcome because you are already invested and now other actions rely on it. When it is on the timetable, it is often easier to just get the job done rather than put it off to rearrange for another time.

The timetable is a powerful mechanism for taking control of our day and living purposefully. Why then, are we reluctant to use it outside of the working day? One reason, as we have discussed is the fact that it is imposed upon us. It is human nature to dislike being told what to do. To add to this, the oldest part of our brain is wired to encourage us to focus on immediacy. This is what used to keep us safe from impending threat. The homo-sapiens who sat around strategizing would have been consumed long ago by opportunistic sabre tooths. Our ancestors were present-biased folk who favoured what is tried-and-tested-going-to-feel-good. Evidentially, this part of our brain does not fully control us or we would still be hunting, gathering and creating cave paintings. However, it is our default setting which we call upon in emergency situations. This explains why it requires so much more effort to strategize. When we try to strategize, our limbic system thinks we are standing in a snake-pit contemplating future bliss. It responds by constantly sending out reminders to pay attention to what is going on around us. It seems that the evolution of our brains has some way to go before we are able to strategize in peace.

Thankfully, we humans have invented a system to upgrade our brains and assist us in this process. Anyone who grew up since the eighties will have watched films or read comic books about cyborgs: half-human, half machine creations, with super strengths or abilities which were supposed to be common place by the early twenty-first century. According to technological humanism: the prophesies are true. Cyborgs really do exist among us. Not only do we frequently use bionic limbs to assist us where the organic counterpart fails, almost all of us have become cyborgs as a means of improving ourselves beyond human capacity. According to modern scientific theories, the actions of humans are governed by a series of algorithms and the fact that we outsourcing many of these to our smart devices means that we are effectively cyborgs already. Think of how you use GPS to get around or your mobile phone to store telephone numbers. From the time when human began to use numbers and writing, our development as a species has jumped forward exponentially. You may not be conscious of it, but you have grown up using an 'external brain'. You need now to set about ensuring that this is used deliberately to increase the capacity of the brain for functions such as capturing, memory and processing.

An organised and conscious external brain is comprised of the first two components of the capturing system outlined in principle one:

- A diary
- A notebook

A Diary

The physical timetable is a visual representation of your habits. Your teaching timetable will present a record of those habits associated with direct teaching because that is the purpose of your job. If you didn't get into the habit of teaching lessons regularly, you would cease to be a teacher. However, it represents a set of routines which operate only in 'normal' circumstances. A timetable is excellent for setting up habits and means you can achieve otherwise insurmountable goals by working on problems a little each week. For example, teaching a pupil to play an instrument by ensuring they have instruction and practice time scheduled for the same day each week. However, if something disrupts this routine, such as a visit from a speaker, a school trip or INSET day, the timetable is considered secondary, only coming into play if nothing else is planned. The interrupting items come from the diary. Diary items are considered sound, constituting real life planning time, relating not to an arbitrary Thursday but to a specific date and time. The diary is your timetable in real time and should form the hard landscape of your day. It acts as a bridge between intention and reality by placing tangible next steps in a realistic place and time. For

109

example, where your timetable states that you have 24 lessons until the big exam, the diary enables you to see exactly how many lessons, as you can discount the 'abnormal' circumstances which would interfere with the teaching of those lessons.

Many organisations persist in distributing paper planners to their staff. However, whilst these are essential in the absence of an alternative, they are outdated in most respects. An electronic diary will allow you the function of repeating events automatically and can also send you reminders and sync events across multiple devices and to all your friends, family and colleagues via email, thereby saving convoluted and often error-ridden correspondence about when a said date will occur. If you choose the software option, it is important that you can access it from your mobile device. The act of entering items you intend to complete forces you to decide when you will get the job done and how long you will spend on doing it. This is crucial to effective processing. It is also useful to have an overview in the front of your diary so you can see your commitments in advance. Diarising is a great way to take into consideration all the factors that otherwise would not have been thought about until the day. Much of the time, your diary will replace your 'to do list' and at least initially, the diary should take precedent over the 'to-do' list. In theory, each day in your diary should detail your priority tasks and how long you will spend doing these.

This may seem like rigid advice at first, especially because if you commit something into your diary it should be with the absolute intention of getting it done. If you put things into your calendar that you might like to do but don't need to do, you won't complete them and you will stop trusting your daily calendar once this happens. However, I am not advising that you stick to your timetable no matter what either. Remember to stick to the principle behind using it to begin with: efficiency. Therefore changes should be made because you have found a more efficient way to use your time, not a less efficient one. Planning ahead gives you the chance to make such judgements in a more grounded way. For example, if you have a very good reason for not marking the homework papers when you arrive to work between 7:00 and 8:00 on Friday morning, then don't do them. However, you should keep in mind that something else has got to give. Marking is a priority task after all and will need to be done sometime soon. This type of thinking will help you to weigh up the task you have chosen not to do up against the task you have chosen to do instead. Do you really need to meet with the parent who just showed up right there and then? If so, when will you do the homework marking and how will this impact the other task you won't do instead? Can you see how sticking to a timetable makes the act of shuffling priorities more of a chore than its worth? You're less likely to reshuffle the whole timetable for the sake of an extra coffee in the staffroom or an extra hour in bed as you are forced to acknowledge what won't get done at the outset rather than waiting for it to become an emergency. As James Clear tells us, our default response is to do what is easy. Therefore if you want to change a bad habit such as not completing the tasks on your timetable, you should make it difficult. Merely by putting in the effort and metal energy required to schedule an action in the first place, you are making it more difficult *not* to do the task which is a step in the right direction. Ultimately, you should aim to make it more difficult *not* to follow your diary than to follow it.

How do you decide what to put in your timetable? This is where your notebook comes in.

A Notebook

Your notebook is the part of your external brain that it is concerned with capturing and storage. It takes passing thoughts from your short term memory and stores them in a place where you can easily access them later. Of the hundreds of thoughts that pass through your mind, many of them are lost within seconds: never to be seen again. Every now and then we catch a thought for a few seconds because we like something about it. It struggles like a butterfly to escape us and most of the time we let it. Mainly this is because we have nothing to put it in whilst we examine it further. Later on, if we even remembered about the butterfly and the urge struck us to draw it - what would be the outcome? A rather sketchy two dimensional drawing with most of the detail and vibrancy lost to the wind. If we wanted to recapture it, we would need to spend time researching similar butterflies on the internet. It seems rather inefficient and time consuming for something which was a fleeting fancy. The resulting drawing may have turned out to be a masterpiece but in reality, how many of us bother to recapture these things? That's the point. So many of our thoughts are like this. It's only the fleeting fancies that come back and revisit us enough to be stored in our long term memory that have any hope of becoming a reality. This is where the notebook comes in. It can help us increase our odds at capturing the ideas that make our practice stand out. Like a diary, notebooks can either be in paper form (like that used by Richard Branson) or electronic. I personally use an electronic diary because like with all things, I always keep in mind one of the two reasons for its use: to capture ideas. An electronic diary does this most efficiently because ideas can be a collection of sound files, images and notes. The notes can be duplicated, shared, organised, reorganised and items can be easily retrieved through search functions. However, there are benefits to both and like with the diary, a paper notebook is vastly better than no notebook. I have a love of notebooks and keep them to use much in the same way I use a bicycle despite owning a car. It's fun and there are other side-effects (such as a different way of thinking when you write long-hand). However, everything I commit to paper notebooks always gets captured digitally. This, I believe is crucial due to the corruptibility of paper files but also because it is important to have files stored in a central place, ready to be accessed later. Hopefully, I've sold you on the digital notebook. If not, there are a number of writers who may do a better job than me.

As well as storing reference material, a notebook should be used to capture actions which require processing. As we discussed, processing requires you to ask the important questions about what will be done with the material. Imagine you have noticed a minor problem with your car and you know you need to get it looked at before it develops into a larger issue. It is tempting to write 'car' on your to-do list. It is brief and therefore practical and in addition, it highlights the central issue at hand. However, if you want it to be dealt with quickly, writing 'car' will not help your case. You may not realise it, but this type of notation will cause you to frequently glaze over and put off the resolution of the item. Why? It is too big. The outcome you want (i.e. your car to be fixed) is at least three steps away and you have not yet decided on your next step. What could be the first step? Calling the garage is fine if you know which garage you want to take your car to and don't want to shop around for quotes (and assuming you have the number for said garage on your phone). However, even in this set of circumstances, you will also need to consider when would be a good time to take your car to the garage. In which case, 'consult diary to find an appropriate date' would be your next step. Now, initially, you may not have been conscious of all the micro-steps involved in making an appointment and may have envisaged a five minute call. However, if you were to go through the whole thought process outline above, up are unlikely to reach the intended step and would end up wasting your five minute window in frustration or indecision. Your unconscious registering of this fact may even cause you to avoid taking any action to begin with. This is how the relatively simple item remains undone on your to-do list. Now consider this: you have completed this and similar items before and know instantly that your first step is 'consult diary to find space for car appointment'. Yes it is more words but it gives you a precise action. Next time you have five minutes you will consult your diary and figure out an appropriate slot. In this way, your to-do items become easy to action immediately. If this were in a digital to-do list, it could now be satisfyingly deleted but you can put a line through a handwritten item with much the same effect.

Ideally, your notebook and diary will work together to provide a framework for your life outside of the timetabled school day. They act as a timetable for all intents and purposes but may lack the clarity and ease of use of a timetable. As James Clear might say, whilst it can be immensely satisfying and easy to use your diary and to do list, it lacks the one vital component necessary to make following it habitual: it is not visible. Imagine you had to pick up a book or open a computer programme to work out what lesson you were teaching next. It would be all too easy to put the book down and forget. It is possible to take this logic one-step further and to create a timetable for your whole working day.

Whilst I appreciate that you may be resistant to this prospect, I would like to share with you my experience of using a visual timetable outside of the school day. My step-daughter and comes to stay for a week over during the half term. She is highly intelligent and has an excellent memory but unfortunately these qualities can work against her because she struggles with anxiety and OCD. At age nine, she developed a fixation with what was happening next and in what order and became very anxious when things unfolded in an unforeseen way. You will understand if you have ever worked with children who suffer from anxiety that such children tend to ask a lot of 'worry questions'. In their quest to gain control over the environment, they also become master manipulators, constantly making 'suggestions' about what actions will make them feel 'safe'. The two combined can become very tiring and difficult to manage, so I drew on my professional experience for resources to use. Having worked with pupils with autism and OCD, I knew that visual timetables were often recommended. I set to work on a timetable which detailed every event for the week all the way up to half-past eight each evening. Initially, my husband balked at the thought of the timetable; surely this sort of thing wasn't practical or necessary? At this, I could sympathise, but as a teacher, I knew it would help. The use of the visual timetable has long since been the domain of schools ever since pupils with a range of neuro-diverse needs have been recognised. As I went to forth to produce the timetable, I experienced the 'resistance': that pull you often get from your primitive brain. The 'resistance' told me it was too much work and it was too complicated getting involved with all the nitty-gritty details well ahead of time. I felt trapped as I knew that once it was committed to the document, it would become far too complicated to change as each decision would have repercussions elsewhere. Furthermore, the nagging voice in my head kept telling me I didn't have the time for all this. Yet I persevered, ignoring all the negative self-talk because unlike my husband, I did not need to ask 'what difference would it make?' for I knew it would make all the difference. And of course it did. The worry questions quickly reduced down to nothing and the persistent requests became unnecessary.

But most interesting of all was the effect that little timetable had on me. I became emancipated from all the minutia which usually crowded my mind during the course of the day. For example, we would be doing one activity and I would be busy calculating what to make for dinner or whether we could get tickets to this or that. Of course, I still had to work all those things out, but as it was a requirement of finishing the task, rather than the antidote to impending doom, I got it all done when I had the chance to focus properly on family time. I had essentially batched my problem-solving and within the confines of real-time, it was all done. I share this story because the process made me reflective about how I was spending my time. It was a nugget of reflection that would not otherwise have been available to me. The week we made the timetable was the first time it occurred to me that I had become a passenger in my own life, achieving all these mundane activities simply because they were on the schedule. I use my timetable for work because my employer insists on it. I complete my timetable for my daughter because it helps her. As a result, all these things will near effortlessly get accomplished. What about *my* priorities? How effortless is it for me to complete them? Surely, if these are my priority tasks, they should be just as easy or easier to complete when they need to get done? Producing a timetable for life ensures that your priorities get seen and dealt with easily and makes it more satisfying when you do. Visibility and reward are two of the cornerstones of building effective habits and after that week, I made the life-changing decision to make a visual timetable a part of my life. It was like a treat to myself, giving me access to all the things I want to achieve at a time when I have the mental energy to both dream them up and commit them to paper. It takes me a matter of minutes to sketch out my week in advance and I enjoy following my timetable as much as I would enjoy boarding a plane to the destination of my dreams. Except rather than travelling in space, the timetable is the vehicle in time which will take me to the things I wish to enjoy in the moment or accomplish in the future. I have many things to thank my step-daughter for, but the power of the visual timetable has been life-changing. An example of an opportunity which arose from ignoring that voice in my head. You too can benefit from the power of the lowly timetable and perhaps rather than passively follow what it tells you to do, you will harness it.

Hopefully, this principle has helped you to appreciate the power you behold, given that planning makes all the difference in everything you do: it is the very difference between the evolved and the eaten. The great news is you are a teacher, planning is not only second nature to you, it is a skill you have perfected over many years. Get smart and use this skill to your full advantage: starting with planning when you will arrive and leave work each day.

PLAN SMART

PRINCIPLE SIX

DON'T STAY LATE

'You should not confuse your career with your life.'

\- Dave Barry

The theme of Principle One was having a clear boundary around your working day. We talked about putting your work in a box and drawing a thick black line around it. However, we cannot avoid the elephant in the room which supposes that staying after hours is an unwritten indicator of a dedicated teacher. We have all worked under or heard stories of the Headteacher who expects staff to stay in the building until 6pm. I once met a Head who proudly told me about her compassion for teachers which she showed by actively discouraging cleaning staff from evicting teachers at 6pm. Teachers want to stay behind, argued the Head, and they should be allowed to do so. I am all in favour of professional freedom, but I would argue that a worrying misconception lies at the heart of the Head's assertion about what makes a satisfied workforce. After all, a leader who is able to manage his or her time will know enough to question the competency of a staff who consistently stay late. Where staying after hours is actively encouraged it would make me question the competency of the leader.

I would argue that consistently staying late at work is an indicator of a disorganised and unproductive worker. For one thing, you are more productive if you give your work clear edges rather than having an open expanse of time in which to complete it. Having a set amount of time forces you to focus only on what is important rather than getting caught up in lots of extraneous details. In other words, leaving work on time will make you *better* at what you do. Even if you are able to prioritise and only complete the most important tasks, Parkinson's law tells us that time is not related to the task at hand in a meaningful way. You bend and shape it, spending as little or as much time as you choose completing the tasks at hand. Just because a car can be assembled from parts in less than an hour, it does not mean that any man can assemble a car from parts in that time, or even that the same man will on every occasion be able to assemble a car in the same amount of time. It is not the time that matters but what we are capable of doing with it.

I have heard plenty of teachers respond to time management advice such as the above with the retort: "Whoever said that obviously wasn't a teacher." One reason for this persistent assumption is rooted in the fact that 'finishing' is considered a rather intangible affair in the profession as was discussed in principle One: *Finished is Better than Perfect*. Another reason stems from the fact that there are certain ingredients required to make the best use of the time available to you such as:

- The energy required to complete the task well
- The appropriate resources to hand
- The mind space required to give you focus
- The necessary information needed to proceed without interruption
- Enough practice at the task that the functional elements are mindless

All of which tend to be particularly scarce resources within an education setting. However, it is important to remember that as scarce as they are in the educational setting, they are likely to be even harder to find in the home. As far as possible you should condense your work into the 8 hours of the day for which you are being paid and reduce your attempts to work at other times. Making advance decisions about *when* you will work and what you will do can enable you to harness the Perato principle and make the most of what you have available to you. Let us first look at the effects of ignoring this advice. When you stay late, you are borrowing time from your down time to pay for the time you did not use well during your work time. It is like going into your overdraft to pay for something you have already consumed because you did not think carefully enough prior to your purchase. However, it is far worse than this, it is using a resource that can never be renewed. Remember: your time is a finite resource and you don't really have that much of it to begin with. You should confront yourself with all the seriousness the matter deserves to ascertain what is causing you to stay late. Two common reasons are: you can't get the work completed during the day; even if you do complete your tasks, you don't feel as though you have been productive enough.

As the bulk of this book is concerned with the first issue (prioritisation and completion of tasks), I will suggest a simple solution to the second reason: get in early instead of staying late.

For reasons we shall see this is not a simple (hour for hour) trade. Think of it like being on a diet and swapping one hundred calories of processed snack foods, for one hundred calories of natural whole foods. At first glance, it may appear to be the same value because the calorie measure is the same but the problem is, you are using a comparison value which does not measure quality. This is key distinction between *real* time and clock time: two hours before work is likely to be multiple times the value of two hours after work for many reasons. Whilst levels of productivity can vary from person to person, it is likely that you will be at your peak during your first few waking hours. Here are some of the benefits to using these hours for your most important work:

121

It Allows You to Plan

In Principle Five we discussed the value of planning ahead but short term real time planning is the most valuable type available to you. A ten minute note about what you will be doing with each period/ work unit of the day with the real limitations before you will give you the overview you need for a really successful start. It will also save you time later in trying to deal with issues you did not foresee whilst you are in the 'thick of it'. Because you will need to check this before you start you day, arguably this type of planning is best done each morning. This will help you take into account unforeseen circumstances such as staff or pupil absence and allows you to create a functional map of the hours ahead.

It Stops You Procrastinating

As we discussed in Principle Two: *Finished is Better than Perfect*, completing any task is satisfying. However, completing a priority task is even more rewarding, filling you with enough energy to take you through the day. Remember this fact, as it can be difficult to imagine the feeling before you get started or even whilst you are working on a task. Your brain will tell you all sorts of lies to try to get you to give up even before you have started. One lie it might try to get you to believe is: it isn't really a priority right now; or it might tell you: it's going to become problematic and I'll never finish it; or I don't have, or even I need… fill in the blank. You might even recognise some of these procrastinations in your students. Learn to anticipate and recognise these responses to make it easier to proceed and carry out your intention.

It sets you up for achieving throughout the day

It is essential that you get the completion feeling as early as possible in the day so that your brain can't lie to you as easily. The way to get the most impact is by completing your most important task first. When I say important, this doesn't usually mean the most urgent, although urgency is sometimes a factor. You'll find that as you get better at managing your time, less things become 'urgent' because your efficiency levels are improving. Important tasks are your principle tasks: planning and marking.

Your mind is clearer at the start of the day

Successful people are the busiest of all, yet they tend to be in the routine of accomplishing their most important tasks *first thing in the morning*. In the morning you are fresh, and your mind is clear. In the afternoon, you are tired and your mind is crammed. Remember from Principle Four: *real* time depends on energy.

You are less likely to be interrupted

Another factor to consider is that early in the morning, the school is likely to be empty, or those who are present are more focussed on their own important tasks. These people have shown a great deal of self-control and intention to earn themselves the additional hour in the day. They are therefore less likely to be looking to waste it and more likely to value your time by not interrupting you. However, make sure you set up your work station away from those who get in just before work, as they seem to be under the impression that not much deep work can be achieved before school 'starts'. In all likelihood, they stayed behind after school to get themselves ready for the following day and can now feel they can enjoy a more relaxed start to the working day. They are looking to have 'words' with people, tell stories or ask questions and will most likely interrupt you unapologetically. If you arrive with these people, your morning time will diminish quickly. Only you can decide whether the activity which used it up is something you value.

You have more will power

Recently, the idea that will-power is a finite resource that is depleted every time we use it has been popularised in time-management Literature. The concept states that every time you make a decision, you are draining your will power, meaning you have less of it left to resist the things that really matter. Thankfully, the theory states that unlike time, will-power can be replenished with rest. This means that when you wake up, your reserves are at their fullest. Recently, the studies upon which this theory has been based have been widely debunked for ignoring contrary evidence; however, it was found that the belief that will power depletes was more powerful than the actual effects. So if you believe that you can only control yourself for so long, you're still probably better off exercising self-control in the morning.

You will encounter less traffic

This advice is true both literally and metaphorically. Getting into work earlier than necessary puts you in the minority. I like to think going anywhere at a different time to the masses is an indicator you are on the path to success - provided it is intentional. After all, it is travelling the unbeaten path that gives us advantages in life. Others may think you are wasting precious energy to complete an unnecessary task; perhaps they don't know what you know.

Depending on the effects of these variables on the value of time, the time before work could be many times the value of the time you stay after work. This means that each day when you wake, you have a window of time to be the most productive you can be. It's remarkable, when you think of it: a superhuman boost when all the stars are aligned happens once every day! Logical, though it sounds, for many of us, morning productivity does not feel natural to many of us. Remember our primitive limbic systems are wired to make us think that if it really was better, then everyone would be doing it. Listen to your pre-frontal cortex on this one: this is about forgoing the present to help you out in the future.

Now you know that getting in early is more beneficial than staying in late, you can no longer explain your choice as a matter of preference. Why would you make the choice to do something which is less beneficial? In all likelihood, it is not a choice to stay late almost every night any more than it is a choice to spend too long on your social-media account. It is a routine which eventually became a habit. This is unsurprising when you understand that humans are wired for repetition. When we fall into habits unconsciously, they tend to stick until we put all our energy into changing them. Football manager, Bobby Robson had it right when he said: 'practice makes permanent'. He understood that repeated action wasn't always about improvement, it was about atomicity. Fortunately, that is not the end of the story, as you know, habits can be reprogrammed quite easily if you understand how they work. Work towards the aim of getting in to your work space at least two hours before the working day to benefit from the power of early work. I would recommend using Charles Duhigg's book: *The Power of Habit* to get you started on creating a habit loop that works for you.

How to use the prime time

What do you accomplish when you first arrive at work?

Most teachers would explain that this time is spent with organisational factors: putting away your things, writing daily information on boards, preparing for subsequent lessons, querying timetabling matters, briefing meetings, coffees and morning duties. It is important that you consider this carefully, because as we discussed earlier, morning time is prime time. The question to ask yourself is whether or not these duties are crucial to your main objective. This does not imply these things are unnecessary or that you should go without them. From my early days as an NQT, I had thought it normal to get to work as early as possible and to stay as late as possible. However when I became a parent working with the boundaries of childcare, I found a job in a small independent Primary school. The nursery which I paid to look after my child would not allow children to be dropped off earlier than 7:30, which meant I didn't arrive to work until 15 minutes before my students. I then needed to leave just twenty minutes after they left. It was then that I realised the truth of the Perato principle. The vast majority of what teachers spend their time doing in the morning contributes to only a small percentage of the results they achieve. As a distracted parent, I was only completing the bare minimum hours. However, the initial guilt subsided quickly as the shorter hours gave me the chance to reflect upon the situation and I concluded that the results I was producing were just as good - if not better than before. The reason, as I understand it now, is that my energy and attention were focused on the crucial areas of concern rather than diluted over the full repertoire of potential concerns. The lack of time had caused me to respect it, using it only for the important tasks. All the other superfluous extras had to be recognised for what they were: distractions and disregarded accordingly. When someone interrupted me during the school day wishing to discuss this or that, a little invisible timer would start off in my head and I would be aware that the decision to have this conversation was a decision not to complete another more important task. When my son grew up, and I was able to get into school early again, I would do so fully aware that this was precious and valuable time. Since those days, the early hours have always been used to complete my most important tasks rather than vague or menial tasks. These are better completed at the planning stage as we shall discuss in Principle Six: Plan smart or throughout the course of the day.

So how do you identify your important tasks? If you have set up your processing system, you will have a list from which to select your tasks. You can refer to Eisenhower's decision matrix to identify urgent and important tasks. Select one to complete. This is your priority task. Priority literally means 'one' and choosing a single task is the only way to truly prioritise. Now you should envisage what the task will look like once it is complete. Never enter a time frame without a plan of how you will use it. Use the prime time at the beginning of the day to decide on the outcomes you want to achieve, without concerning yourself with the 'nitty gritty' of how you will do this. The list of outcomes will need to be placed somewhere you can see it most of the time such as a large dry wipe board so they can be rubbed off as you complete them. When you are in the flow of the working day you will solve any practical problems that arise as long as you can keep referring back to the list of outcomes. When immersed in the practical functions required to respond to the needs of your pupils, your brain is too preoccupied to remember your own priorities which is why they so often get neglected.

Break the habit of staying late

However, you must also break your habit of staying late or you will be tempted to tell yourself that you could complete even more work by getting in early *and* staying late. Don't forget to focus on the true purpose of your work rather than on the work itself. If you are to fulfil the purpose of your job, it is essential that you take a step back and reflect on your productivity: the efficiency with which you meet your purpose on a daily basis. From the moment we wake up, the most crucial thing we can do is visualise our aims for the end of the day so we can prioritise. As Stephen Covey says: "The main thing is to keep the main thing the main thing."

The method for success is twofold: first visualise the end of the day and second: create a routine to strengthen the power of this image. As James Clear in Atomic Habits points out, it is the second step - the systems which lead to us actually achieving desired outcomes. If you don't embed the systems, you are doomed to watch your vision fail, as whilst you have the will to change, you don't have the means. A powerful approach to the two-step process is to combine both steps. Instead of simply visualising leaving early, try to script your leaving work routine, working backwards from your ideal leave time much like you would if you had a set arrangement and then rehearse the sequence of events in your mind. Working backwards is so effective because it does the important calculations about when to begin tasks related to leaving ahead of time. These tend to get ignored until it is too late because they require more brain power than you would have spare when engrossed in a last minute task.

Whilst you are happy to make this effort when you have a dentist appointment to get to, you may feel that this is 'overkill' for a regular day and requires far too much energy than necessary. If this is the case, you should question the assumption about why appointment yourself should not be treated with the same seriousness as an appointment with someone else. Unfortunately we tend to be far too complacent about borrowing time from ourselves or those we love. We may intend to but rarely pay back the time, forcing ourselves and loved-ones to become what Erin Dion author of 'Time Management Ninja' refers to as 'residual beneficiaries' – the ones who get whatever is left after the spoils of an estate after all more important obligations and debts have been paid off. If you think of it, this behaviour is highly illogical as we wouldn't keep our hairdresser waiting for even ten minutes if we can avoid it; yet staying behind at work entails keeping our children, spouses and our own aspirations waiting at home for us. Scripting your end-routine should be much the same as your morning routine which (I assume) gets you to work in good time every morning. When you script your routine, it is important not to be too generous with the time allotted for getting ready as you will more than likely become tempted to complete 'just one more task' at the last minute bringing you back to square one again. A suggested routine might go something like this:

1. Save your digital documents
2. Review completed and pending tasks - adding to your to-do list for tomorrow
3. Turn off your computer
4. Pack your bag with one task (one set of books to mark/ one policy to read)
5. Place your bags by the door, whilst you return to clear your desk, set the classroom for tomorrow (e.g. writing the date on the board or any questions to get your pupils thinking as soon as they enter)

If you repeat your end of day routine enough times, then each action will lead naturally to the other, and you are less likely to get pulled off schedule. Just like your morning routine, you want your evening routine to become so natural that you find yourself walking out of the building mindlessly at roughly the same time each day.

At first be prepared to feel insecure, rushed and as though you have forgotten something. Try to remember that anxiety is a natural response to a change in routine and see it as a sign that you are on to a good thing. It can help to get in the habit of conducting regular productivity reviews throughout the day. Are you on track to complete your priority tasks? What changes can be made to realign you with your goals? This will help you to close your mental loops in advance of leaving. Whenever you remember, always treat the end of the day as your deadline. There are a number of habits you can adopt to make this principle a reality in your working day.

Schedule appointments at the end of the school day

It can help if you schedule regular appointments for the end of each day. This is more easily done if you have children in childcare provisions. I found that becoming a working parent helped me to significantly improve my time management. I was getting far more done in a short space of time, simply because I had to. Taking work home became a useless exercise and so wasn't an option which forced me to focus on the bare essentials. If you don't have children, book your exercise, hair and medical appointments at this time. Try to do all your errands after you teaching hours rather than leaving them to do on Saturday mornings. This means you will have to leave work as early as possible to get to the bank/ post-office/ supermarket before it closes. It has the added benefit of restricting work of all types to the working week, reserving weekends for more meaningful activities.

Tell others what time you intend to leave

If you intend to leave early, it is important that others know what time you intend to leave. This should prevent the last minute 'have you got a minute' chats during your end of day routine. However, if such chats occur anyway, you should begin your routine as soon as possible - your routine will take much longer than normal if someone is simultaneously speaking in your ear. The benefit of having told them in advance that you intend to leave is that you shouldn't feel guilty about getting ready whilst they are still talking to you.

Don't cheat by simply taking work home

This can be even less efficient than completing it at work and also takes away the need to prioritise in much the same way as staying behind at work. The only time you should take work home is if you have planned to do so in advance, whether because it is best completed in your home environment or because it is compensating from some time that you know you will lose in the future due to an additional meeting or some other essential hands on activity.

Ideally work taken home should never be work that you failed to complete during your normal work hours. If you cannot complete a certain activity in work hours you should cut down on the amount of time it takes you to complete (do it quicker) or ditch, delegate or defer it until it goes away. Remember to have a bias for completion, which requires you to reflect in advance on the outcome you would like and how this can be achieved in the allotted time. As we have discussed, there are only three tasks that are important enough to even consider doing at home. These are planning, teaching and feedback. Teaching can be taken home to complete in advance (e.g. by producing an exciting film for your pupils). You can then complete another task whilst they watch the fruits of your labour. This is an offset of labour which could prove particularly fruitful if the value of the lesson is greater than if you had

131

taught in situ. Do make sure you limit the time spent in production if you want this to count. Marking and planning can also be completed at home, however, unless you limit the time you spend doing these, the offset to time is much less likely to be like-for-like. You want an hour of your time spent planning or marking to increase the value of your teaching time by at least the same amount. Otherwise it becomes useless. I would recommend getting into the habit of completing both planning and marking during work hours. This will help you to plan only that which is made better by planning and to mark in a way that will best lead to progress. However, if you find yourself taking one of these tasks home, I would suggest it be your marking. It may be necessary to take marking home from the last lesson of the day if you have plans to leave early as it should always be marked at the first opportunity. However, you can always complete it during your 'before school time' rather than transport the books home. The act of lugging around takes time and energy away from the actual task at hand. If you take home marking, always limit it to one set of marking (e.g. books or papers from one lesson) as this will require much less mental energy to complete as the repetition will take up some of the strain. So why not take planning home instead? After all this is far less cumbersome? Three reasons why you should take home marking rather than planning have been outlined below:

1. Marking is very visual and tends to be linked to physical objects. It can therefore be easy to set and work to limits. On the other hand, planning lacks clear edges. It is possible to finish planning more quickly and easily than marking but because it varies a great deal with respect to both the planner and the task at hand it can often be viewed as 'open-ended'. In general, it is best to avoid viewing any essential tasks as 'open-ended'

and also best to avoid completing any task viewed in this way outside the normal working day.

2. The working day tends to be comprised of our highest energy hours and planning requires higher brain capacity than marking because - even if you batch it - it is comprised of lots of different tasks. You are therefore going to complete relatively less planning than marking in the same amount of time. You are also likely to make more mistakes and waste time correcting these.

3. Planning is better when you are in the immediate environment in which the tasks will take place as there are considerations and inspiration to be gained from your surroundings. Also you will have access to any larger resources and be able to better visualise the situation. On the other hand, written feedback is relative only to the physical work upon which you write the comments and this can usually be transported.

Think like a Supply Teacher

One curious way to do overcome the urge to stay late is to think like a supply teacher. Supply teaching is an interesting phenomena. Any teacher who has experienced both contract teaching and supply teaching, either first or second hand will recognise the startling difference between both types of work. The output appears similar: students are kept busy with an activity and some form of output is produced. However, the teacher's attitude is entirely different. The supply teacher, who is getting paid by the hour, arrives with very little time to spare prior to the lesson. He or she is concerned with fulfilling the objectives of the regular teacher, who more often than not, sets this out in the form of an 'activity' for the students to complete rather than a skill or piece of knowledge for them to acquire. Once the activity is complete, the outcomes are recorded, the work may be marked to a surface level and the supply teacher leaves, careful to do so as soon as possible following the end of the lesson. The purpose for working seems to be almost entirely selfish and they exert the absolute minimum of energy necessary to achieve those ends. Everyone knows that the supply teacher does not get paid for the holidays but if you actually calculate the amount earned for every hour you actually work, you may find that supply teaching works out to be significantly more lucrative. Yes the supply teacher's objective for working will differ from yours but that should not stop you making a link between the time you expend and your impact. The supply teacher stops work at a certain time because at this time, he or she ceases to be able to generate an income. You should recognise the time at which you cease to be able to improve learning through that particular action. For example: the smart planner will recognise that some planning will facilitate learning better than no planning but lots of planning will not necessarily increase the effect. Moreover, too much planning will start to hinder your ability to facilitate learning. As a result you may become so preoccupied with the plan that you lose sight of the affect it was designed to have. In theory, you could reach the stage where you waste time teaching pointless lessons, just because you have planned them. A mind-exercise to help you get to grips with the delicate balance between effort and impact is to view teaching as though you were a child. You want it to be fantastic, but you want to get it done so you can get on to the next thing. Ask yourself: what's the least amount of work you can do to get the same output?

A supply teacher is forced into this situation. He or she has to achieve an objective and if he or she does so, the job has been done. However, there are no hours after lessons for planning and none after for marking. The employer has made this clear in his or her payment structure. The supply teacher may not even be paid for the lunch hour and therefore should not work during this time. Breaks are for eating, phone calls and toilet breaks. And yet, the supply teacher is still expected to teach and the work still needs to be marked. So how does he or she perform this impossible feat? The same way the pupils in a primary school class are capable of producing an artistic masterpiece or a complete story within a single lesson when we imagine it would take weeks to accomplish the same. The good supply teacher, for the time she is paid, is focussed only on the task for which he or she is paid. True to Parkinson's Law, precisely because she is expected to complete the task within the allotted time, she does so.

Be Psychologically Prepared

No matter what you do, your job needs to have physical boundaries or an incessant desire to 'get more done' will spread out as far as you will let it. Any professional who is not restricted by shifts may find it difficult to put in place such boundaries unless they make it a matter of principle. For better or for worse, teachers tend not to have their start and finish times made explicit. Time spent actively teaching is restricted by a student timetable (for primary teachers by the amount of hours in which children are in the premises). However, compulsory meetings, extra-curricular expectations and parents' evenings can mean that the timetable tends to bear little resemblance to actual time spent working. Exactly why this situation persists is difficult to define but it is safe to say that the institution itself is not wholly responsible for this state of affairs. It is often the teachers themselves who not only allow the situation to persist but actively facilitate the boundless work day in their day-to-day practice.

There are likely multiple fears and motivations which make it difficult for the teacher let go at the end of the school day. One may be a sense of fear of getting behind or a sense of the pursuit of getting ahead. In these cases, the misguided choice has been caused by losing sight of purpose. Whilst the work was initially pursued for a conscious reason, without proper reflection time and systems in place, the purpose is lost and the work ends up being pursued for its own sake. In much the same way, the misguided capitalist comes to pursue money for its own sake, forgetting the initial reasons she came to want it to begin with. Moreover, the law of diminishing returns tells us that it is possible to tip the balance to the point where the work stops aiding and actually begins to hinder the purpose for which it was intended. Some free time is necessary to unwind and help you feel happy but too much can make you bored and therefore reduces your happiness. Some work is necessary to help students learn faster, too much will hinder your ability to do this effectively. It is possible to identify when the balance has been tipped by paying attention to how what we are doing makes us feel. Behaviour that is undertaken for a purpose feels very different to that undertaken without purpose. Just as we know that a certain amount of relaxation time is necessary to unwind and help you feel happy, we are sensitive to the feeling that too much can make you bored and uncomfortable. In the same way, we should be aware of how much work is necessary to help students learn faster and when the balance has been tipped, beginning to hinder your ability to do this effectively. Learning to use the prime time effectively provides the ultimate failsafe for this pitfall as it allows you begin at the start with mental clarity and purpose in mind. Those who use the morning hours benefit from the mental space and physical freedom to identify their important tasks before they get consumed by what is urgent. By finishing when you know these tasks have been completed, you give yourself the mental space to pursue other things, ready to re-engage with the purpose of your work for the next day. Abiding by the principle of not staying late allows you to 'see the wood for the trees'.

When you finish teaching your last lesson for the day, look at the work and decide what you will do as a result of the output from that lesson. Then get out of the building. That's your essential marking, teaching and planning done for the day; anything else is like placing an over-priced bow on the top of an already expensive gift. It may feel and look satisfying but it doesn't add to the present and more crucially - it will ultimately end up in the bin. As you know by now, you are using a resource that can never be renewed. Use this principle to put it to good use and never take more than you need.

.

PRINCIPLE SEVEN

BATCH YOUR TASKS

'Nothing is particularly hard if you divide it into small jobs.'

-   Henry Ford

On December 1st 1913, Henry Ford's assembly line first started rolling. With the revolutionary effect of speeding up production and driving down costs, this was the earliest example of wide scale batching in the manufacturing industry. Since the time of the industrial revolution, the use of assembly lines has drifted into business of all types and the principle has been generally accepted as the most efficient way to get things done. Ford was famous for his obsessive examination of every detail of the manufacturing process in a similar way to the way Ben Hunt-Davis examined every action completed by his rowing team. Instead of 'Will it make the boat go faster?' he asked, 'Will it make a car quicker?' He even examined of unnecessary steps his workers had to take during a day's work so as many physical movements as possible led to production. They repeated the same task hundreds of times per day and as Ford argued, it released them of the need to think: a side effect for which he claimed most people were grateful.

A type of batching known as task batching is today being used as a clever productivity hack, in which all the thinking is done in advance and actions of the same type are completed one after the other within a designated timeslot without interruptions. The important protected time element allows you the focus required to inhabit real time. This means you can complete even the most complex tasks in much less time and with the minimal expenditure of mental energy. For many years, sexist banter has degraded men for not being able to multitask as well as women. Now evidence suggests that far from being the subject of ridicule, being able to concentrate on just one thing and ignore everything else is actually a sought-after skill. We now understand that those who try and do it all are actually less effective, less accurate and ironically less productive than their more single-minded counterparts. As we discussed in Principle Two, when we try to multitask, we have too many channels open at once and end up switching rapidly between them and consuming all the energy required for the task. Batching is essentially the antithesis of multi-tasking: which involves completing as many tasks as possible at any given time. It too involves an attempt to complete multiple tasks but these are completed one at a time in quick succession and they are all on the same channel, preventing the need to change the mental or physical resources required for each task.

One common example of a task-batch is batching food preparation. When my husband began his body building diet, it required he eat four cooked meals per day. Like many others on a carefully controlled diet, batching was the only sensible option and he set about preparing all his meals for the next three days in advance. Laborious and time consuming at first, the chore took an hour and a half of his time. Each time he undertook the process, it became faster until within a few months it was taking half the time - around the same amount of time it took to cook a single evening meal. The act of batching actually multiplied the value of his time. So how did the whole come to be greater than the sum of the parts? The time he gained back was from a collection of intangible factors such as refined skill, more efficient systems, the power of momentum and increased focus. When you allow 45 minutes to prepare an evening meal, only a very small proportion of that time is actually spent actively cooking. Much of the time is spent in preparation, some in interruptions (e.g. emptying the bin) and a surprising amount in organizing the utensils required for food preparation. You will likely be distracted and your focus drawn towards other matters. When you batch-cook, the preparation, organization, distractions and interruptions will still occur of course, but they only occur once. This can mean that the preparation of twelve meals takes around the same time as preparing two, leading to enormous time-savings in the future (not to mention the financial savings associated with this type of efficiency).

Batching in this way can be a useful habit for teachers to engage in during the holidays, making it easier to have a proper rest without unfinished work persisting as a kind of unfinished background noise whilst you try to relax. If you intend to get some planning and organizing completed for the term ahead, try planning a 'staycation' where you batch planning for one day and organization for another. You can work in short bursts using the Pomodoro technique or longer stints with breaks which take you to a different channel, such as a walk in nature or a chat with a friend. As well as the time savings, you will also benefit from gaining momentum, focus and increased skill-level. In addition, the processes of batching planning and organization gives you the benefit of seeing the bigger picture. When you do this, Parkinson's Law will encourage you to simplify a task to its most basic and crucial components rather than fleshing it out with unnecessary detail to fill the time available.

However, to be effective at this technique will require increased reserves of will power to get started. You should be prepared to meet what is known in the productivity world as the Resistance. Unlike the piecemeal approach of completing a variety of shorter tasks interspersed with breaks, the reality of batching is that it means you are standing in the shadow of one big mountainous task which can be such a daunting prospect that it can prevent you getting started. It is one thing to say 'I will spend an hour or so planning a lesson' and quite another to say you intend to spend at least an entire day planning an entire unit of work in one go. This is compounded by the fact that only a tiny portion of the task will appear urgent, as the vast majority of the task will be concerned with the far of future and our present bias means we fail to acknowledge its importance.

One way to overcome this potential barrier is appreciating the power of associations between location and the type of work you do. In the above example, the will-power problem can be overcome by making the journey to work to complete the planning. The benefit of physically moving oneself to a specific space with the intention of completing a task there is powerful in itself: the action of getting out the door is an automatic motion and comprises the daunting first step. Once in progress, you can switch off until you get there, knowing the wheels are in motion towards achieving your intended outcome. In addition, the process of entering the work space will automatically activate the mindset you need to get going without any additional effort on your part. As soon as you arrive, you need to stay focused on your intended outcome by visualizing it: e.g. actually picture looking at your finished plans for the half term with the resources you need in allocated boxes. This will stop you getting tempted by other distractions as you walk into the work environment and help you recognize clearly when you are 'finished' and it is time to go home. As well as using the association between place and task, other associations like a select piece of music can instantly put your brain in the correct frame of mind or channel for completing the task at hand.

However, during term time, our practice is comprised

of a number of high priority tasks which are often urgent and must be dealt with as they arise. Therefore, regularly reinforced single task slots are likely to be much harder to come by. Arguably is not possible for a teacher to batch 'dealing with pupil problems' or 'after school clubs' and teachers are required to fulfil regular externally scheduled obligations such as break duty or staff meetings, none of which will necessarily connect with our priorities but all of which require our full attention. However, there are actually several areas of the teaching profession which not only lend themselves to 'batching' but already involve batching at a systemic level. Again, when you focus only on the most vital units of the profession: planning, teaching, feedback, we find that each of these areas rely on batching on a fundamental level. They are so fundamental that perhaps we miss them.

Batching in Teaching

We mustn't forget that batching is built into the very fabric of our education system as students are batched according to their levels of development. Groups of students are sent up to the next 'level' of learning each year until they leave our institution, all the while their places being filled by new batches rising up through the ranks. This means there is no need to consider age or years of school experience too carefully when planning lessons as this basic consideration is already built into the system. Yes, we get het up about 'August born' pupils in early education but we tend to take for granted that the pupils we teach all have a similar level of life and school experience and therefore waste virtually no mental energy on this consideration at the planning stage.

Batching in Feedback

Perhaps the second most obvious area in which batching is systemic in education is in the mass production of feedback. We are often dealing with tens or even hundreds of individuals requiring feedback within a similar timeframe; if we didn't batch it, it simply wouldn't get done. You are probably familiar with task batching as being the most effective way to complete marking and annual reports. Parents' evenings are another form of feedback batching which seems curious if you deconstruct it. We ask parents to come all the way in to school twice a year for just a five or ten minute conversation about their child in which we are expected to discuss their progress over a term or more. However, given the ratio of students to teachers and the number of hours in the day, we recognise that it is simply the only way to ensure that such conversations happen fairly and regularly.

Batching in Planning

As we discussed in Principle Five, timetables are the most basic planning unit for teachers. They have the benefit of ensuring you are in the right place both mentally and physically when you complete all actions of a particular type. The principle of batching is embedded in the use of timetables as these are used to concentrate certain types of activities into a specific unit of time and then repeating them at precise intervals. This practice is commonly known as 'time-boxing' and is essentially the act of coupling chunks of time with a specific type of activity. When you group distinct actions or types of actions in this way, they can be performed with pre-prepared mental or physical resources. In a similar way to the effect of a physical location, you're the appropriate mental channel can be activated much more quickly if you practice the same activity at regular time intervals. This is because the momentum required to get started is diminished each time you revisit the activity until eventually you are ready to go whenever you enter that specific timeslot. This makes the inhabitants of the timeslot receptive to the relevant behaviours needed to complete the task well without expending extra energy attempting to cultivate these each time. Cal Newport, author of 'Deep Work' explains how channel batching or the 'rhythmic philosophy' as Newport names it, can lead to faster improvements in learning, based on the law of incremental gains. By completing tasks a small amount at a time at regular intervals over a sustained period, habits are ingrained more deeply and mistakes are minimized. Furthermore, as a happy side-effect, progress becomes effortless as you are always building on what was achieved before. Taking this into account it is clear that the use of timetables in education is more than just a logistical nicety: it is pedagogically powerful.

When you consider it carefully, you will see that teaching in the mainstream education system is essentially a grand-scale batching exercise: designed with efficiency in mind. So perhaps it is not so farfetched to find examples of where batching can assist with time management in all areas of the profession. If you can see it for what it is and appreciate its usefulness, you can use batching to your advantage every day. For example, if you want to batch a complex task such as planning, you can draw on the production line model and strip the task down to its more fundamental units to identify which is the most essential unit, as this is what will drive all the others. Next, complete as many repetitions of that unit as possible. For example, when it comes to planning, the most obvious place to begin is at the most fundamental tenet of the lesson: the learning objective. Usually learning objectives are written in the context of entire learning plans as this seems to embed them in the relevant context. This also means that the writing of the objective can get pulled here and there during the planning process through consideration of additional and sometimes extraneous details. Batching forces you to remain focused on the most essential part of the process: it is essentially the only way you can be aware you are on task. As we touched on in Principle Five, planning with the end in mind is the most efficient way to overcome obstacles and achieve what is important. The learning objective should be predefined, it is the lesson which should be adapted to suit it. Write all your learning objectives in advance as this will help you to view lessons from a skill-development rather than a 'coverage' perspective. When you view long term lesson planning in terms of 'what do I need the students to know by the end of the (lesson/unit/year/)?' you are beginning with the end in mind, which helps you to find the most efficient way to achieve the objectives, rather than getting caught up in the activities at hand.

To harness the power of channel batching, you just need to extend the timetabling principle already embedded in your daily practice to other activities as well as meetings and lessons. Then protect these units of time for only these activities. In the same way as when you begin a lesson, as you enter the particular timeframe, a channel will open and completing the type of task you need to get done will happen fluidly. Once you are 'in the swing' of whatever the task is, the hard part is over and you are able to maximize the timeframe. One way to put this principle to good use is to be specific about the type of activity allocated to a specific PPA slot on your timetable. For example, pledge to dedicate period three on Wednesday to marking. This allows you to identify your priority for that one particular slot every week. Psychologically, this is a very powerful thing: once you know your priority and can focus on it exclusively in real time, nothing else matters. This is when things get done.

The next principle is all about the single most common thing teachers tend to batch: written feedback.

TIME MANAGEMENT TEACHER

PRINCIPLE EIGHT

MARK SMART

'If you need a machine and don't buy it, then you will ultimately
find that you have paid for it and don't have it.'

-   Henry Ford

Marking has long since been considered a staple of teaching but expectations surrounding this practice has changed significantly over the years. At the time of writing, there has been a movement away from the pressure which previously existed to complete large amounts of written feedback. In 2019, a review of teacher workload was undertaken by an independent board which examined a number of factors contributing to a growing consensus that teacher workload was becoming unmanageable. The study focussed on marking and seems to be based on a number of commonly held assumptions about this practice, namely:

1. The central purpose of marking is to provide evidence of teaching.
2. Many pupils don't read marking.
3. There is little evidence to suggest that the practice of deep marking leads to improved progress.

Those undertaking the study found that marking makes relatively little difference so long as some form of feedback occurs as part of a lesson. Ultimately, they concluded that most of the marking which takes place is essentially a waste of the teacher's time. In response, many schools have adapted their policies to state that whilst most lessons should include some form of feedback, there will not be an expectation to produce written feedback. If you work in a school with a relaxed attitude to marking, I urge you to take a long-sighted view of the situation. Take the time to weigh up the potential benefits of not marking with the potential cost to progress in each case. Guidance can and will change, ultimately you want to ensure your practice is consistent with your values. Arguably, eliminating written feedback certainly would go a significant way towards improving a teacher's work-life balance. However, so would eliminating teaching: we must be wary of a false economy.

Unfortunately, whilst it not be what we want to hear, resolving the work load problem is not as simple as the school saying 'we don't expect you to mark'; if we don't give our pupils adequate feedback, we will have to pay for this in other ways. The Department for Education's preoccupation with the time consuming nature of marking may be concealing a much bigger problem: that is teacher time being consumed with affairs which are far less significant to our purpose. Whilst many schools have adopted a radically lighter approach to marking, you will be hard pushed to find these teachers skipping home early to spend time with their families. We must bear in mind that whatever the motivation for bringing the findings of this study to your intention, the affect is likely not that you spend less time at work, but that you have less grounds not to spend time on other work-related tasks.

If you are no longer *expected* to mark, then you can no longer use this as a legitimate excuse for not performing other tasks in the time originally allotted for this purpose. Can you be sure this result will not adversely affect your ability to perform as a teacher? Whilst the policy will state that you don't need to mark, it will not state that you should not mark. You must actively ask yourself whether you can achieve the same results for your pupils without marking. If marking books *is* the most efficient way to facilitate pupil progress, then if you relinquish this practise, you will be creating more work for yourself rather than less. We are skilled professionals, able to challenge policy from the ground up, so I encourage you to carefully consider each of the arguments against the practice of marking.

The central purpose marking is to provide evidence of teaching

The practice of marking work began at a time before it was checked by inspectors. Much like other staples of our education system, it was introduced as the most efficient means available to complete one of the core parts of the job: for teachers to offer pupils the feedback they need to help them learn. Not to show anyone that a teacher has looked at each piece of work. Not to demonstrate that teachers have spent many additional hours on the job. Not because we have been told to. However, it seems like so many things in life, we have strayed so far from the original purpose of marking that it has come to be pursued for its own sake. I know a teacher – the type of person who will likely continue working long hours without expecting any additional remuneration his whole career. He told me proudly of his stoic attempts to reconcile the situation by essentially 'Doubling up' his marking i.e. giving your verbal feedback to the pupil at the time and then later writing a similar or less detailed version of the comment when he later comes to mark the books. On such occasions, verbal feedback is good use of your time: it is giving information to the student to help them learn faster; whereas the written feedback is poor use of your time, being completed only for the purpose of *showing* you have fed back, but losing much of the richness of the original comment. One set of feedback for the student, a second set for the senior leader. If you are giving written feedback in this manner, I would agree with the anti-marking movement and argue that yes, you are wasting your time. However, first, I would ask you to be honest with yourself: do you really give personalised verbal feedback to *every* student? How can you be sure? One of the benefits of written feedback is that the physical work acts as a written record of your feedback, ensuring you have seen every piece of work. It is likely, therefore that 'doubling up' (i.e. giving both verbal and written feedback to a pupil) will only occur in a minority of cases. Where verbal feedback did not occur, written feedback can legitimately take its place. In the small number of cases where verbal feedback *has* taken place, it is possible to combine this with a written record of said feedback. This should not be 'doubling up' if it is done for the purpose of reinforcing your message (rather than proving it has taken place). Simply jot down a comment which will serve to remind the student of the learning point you made or create a written activity to consolidate.

Many pupils don't read marking

There are two ways that pupils not reading marking has been connected to the conclusion that marking doesn't work. One states that pupils do not read the marking *because* it doesn't lead to progress. Another states that pupils do not read the marking and *therefore* it does not lead to progress. Pupils may not read marking but it is illogical to deduce that this is *because* marking doesn't lead to their making progress. The decision not to read the comment is unlikely to be the result of reasoned judgement. Not reading a comment – particularly when it will likely lead to further effort on the part of the reader is the path of least resistance. We are all prone to taking this path unless we are motivated by a reward or we are making a reasoned judgement. If you think about it, effective feedback *should* challenge a student. The more effective the marking, the less likely a student is to want to read it, because doing so will involve cognitive work. The same cognitive work required to make progress.

Likewise it is a fallacy to suggest that pupils don't read the marking and therefore it doesn't work. This is tantamount to saying that offering verbal feedback to pupils is pointless because they never listen anyway. Just as with all things that fail to happen naturally, marking requires that you set expectations and consistently reinforce them if you intend for them to have an effect. If your pupils don't read your marking, it is usually for one of two reasons:

a) You don't expect them to
b) You don't mark consistently enough

Not for any more esoteric reason related to the effectiveness or non-effectiveness of written feedback.

There is little evidence to suggest that the practice of 'deep' marking leads to improved progress

There is little evidence to suggest that our education system is effective at all. And yet we still continue to perpetuate its norms and to adapt to its policies. Conversely, you don't need evidence to tell you what happens if you don't regularly mark your books. You will have already found that some students will continue plugging away, producing beautiful, high quality work. These are the 'ideal' intrinsically motivated students which many educators have in mind when creating policy. You will already know that many students will not only fail to make progress, they will go backwards, failing to put in the effort required to meet even the minimum standard. These students are the externally motivated lot for whom school is a place which they must attend and for whom quality checks must be in place. From these students, the

153

unmarked work will be untidy, inaccurate and even inexplicably absent when left unchecked. It could be argued that 'not marking' is not the same as 'not looking at' work. A teacher could spend much less time simply quality checking the work and asking students to redo or edit work that is not up to standard. However, if you think about this concept, a teacher will need to make a note to remind him/her which students need to edit which pieces of work. Arguably such a record is best placed on the relevant work as this places the onus for the next action in the *student*'s rather than your own in-tray. What of the students who *do* complete the work to the expected standard? What purpose has it achieved? How will it be further improved?

Those students whose quality of work improves when they know you are checking their work are motivated by the act of marking. This may be uncomfortable to acknowledge as we generally assume that extrinsic motivation is 'bad' and intrinsic motivation is good. However, according to Charles Duhigg, these extrinsically motivated students are not at all unique. They are just like us. The scientific explanation is that we all rely on 'habit loops' to accomplish most of what we do in life. A habit loop is a series of actions is formed by the most basic part of our brains and happens without our conscious awareness. These loops will begin with a trigger and will need to be closed if we are to reinforce the behaviour. For those tasks we do not find enjoyable in themselves, the reward needs to be something extrinsic. This does not need to be lavish but can be as simple as acknowledgement from another. If the 'reward' is removed, the cycle is broken and the behaviour, no longer positively reinforced, will cease to occur. Of course we all have at least one self-reinforcing behaviour which does not rely on an extrinsic reward but is enjoyable to us: an end in itself. However, it is highly unlikely that this will be true of each student for each task you expect of them. This fact is especially true when you push students beyond their comfort zones as you encourage them to constantly improve. Therefore, if you want the behaviour to become a habit, you have to close the loop in the most efficient way possible. This is one of the key reasons we use feedback: acknowledgement. In order to meet educational outcomes, teachers need students to comply with activities they do not find inherently rewarding, so written feedback - which was literally attached to the activity they had completed became the reward.

The reward trick is based on a manipulation of the oldest part of our brains: the limbic system. It works in a similar way to reinforcing the behaviour of animals by consistently offering a treat each time the behaviour is repeated. Perhaps it is for this reason that many educationalists are keen to move away from systems which indicate that a pupil's motivations lie elsewhere than in the classroom. Maybe it gives them the creeps to think we have successfully captured millions of humans and trained them to perform particular behaviours against their will. For many, the fact that our students rely on extrinsic rewards can be an uncomfortable truth. It speaks volumes about the nature of the education system and even further into the nine-to-five culture into which many of the students you teach will be fed. I once attended a CPD session led by a teacher at a school who had abandoned all external rewards and sanctions on the basis that they diminished the impact of intrinsic rewards. The teacher finished the session by announcing that after an exhausting day they were looking forward to getting home and having a nice glass of wine.

The age-old question of how to cultivate internal motivation in people (and yet still get them to perform in a specific way) is a much more fundamental concern which exceeds the scope of this book. However, even if we could cultivate internal motivation, we mustn't fall into the trap of thinking this removes the need for meaningful feedback. Feedback is an essential part of life – even for the intrinsically motivated. Intrinsic motivation is very important but this only takes us so far; if you keep working hard but feel as though your hard work is not recognised, eventually you will plateaux or even fall backwards. Moreover, students need to learn about the power of feedback and how to use it effectively. Consider the intrinsically motivated student who does not learn to expect extrinsic feedback. He will work dutifully for his employer but will never request a pay-rise or demand 'What's in it for me?' Sound like anyone you know? Feedback is as much for the student who *always* works hard as it is for the student who simply won't bother unless she knows you will check.

As well as acknowledgement and reinforcement, feedback is essential for the purposes of quality-checking or assessing the work. Feedback from assessment comes in two main forms: summative and formative. With summative assessment, the marking is quick, anonymous and systematic: the analysis is where the feedback happens and this is where focus should lie. With formative assessment, a qualitative approach is taken to the marking of the work and the feedback is given as swiftly as possible. The key to maintaining efficiency is in spending the time at the relevant stage of the process and automatizing the remaining steps.

Summative Feedback

Whilst formative assessment provides feedback to students, summative assessment provides feedback to the teacher: it should be conducted as a means to spot check our own practice and correct as necessary. The use of summative data, if executed effectively will ultimately lead to progress, which is why minimal time should be spent on the actual marking part and maximum time should be spent on the important part: *responding* to the data. We must keep in mind that this is the ultimate end product and swiftly complete the summative marking part so we can get to the important end product: planning in response to our analysis.

The most common example of this is marking test papers. Usually these are completed at the end of a unit of work to test an outcome but can also be done intermittently to gauge our effectiveness at teaching particular units, such as spellings or a pop-quiz. Once the test has been completed, it is important to establish an effective system to maintain efficiency.

Establish a Logical System

Put the test papers in alphabetical order before you start. It is good practice to use register order wherever possible but this is particularly helpful when inputting data into a spreadsheet. The best way to do this is to ensure they are always collected in alphabetical order. When you enter the data (or delegate this manual task to someone else), the job takes only seconds rather than minutes.

Mark Systematically

The quickest way by far to mark test papers is to mark them a page at a time. First have all the papers in a pile with the first page facing the front. Look at the answer then check this with the test paper. Once the page is marked, turn it over so that the next page is revealed but then mark the next paper in the same way as the first. By the time you reach the fourth paper, you are likely to have memorised the relevant answers so the process is much quicker, becoming almost mechanical towards the end of the pile. You now have a new pile, all facing the correct way to mark the next set of questions and you can begin the process again. Processing papers in this way means you are dealing with the data alone; unless you constantly flick to the cover page, you will have no immediate grasp of the particular student's areas of difficulty. Summative assessment is controlled, with answers taken on their own merit based on a set of pass or fail criteria; they aren't supposed to be contextualised. Judgements about what 'we know' the student meant will only conflict with the marking criteria. This will cause a decision paralysis which will slow the whole process down. This is why standardised assessment is marked by an external examiner.

Complete a Test Analysis

Summative marking doesn't necessarily entail you don't know anything about the student's strengths and weaknesses. Once it is completed, you can complete a test analysis grid as part of the process. If this has not already been provided with the testing resource, you can make your own by recording the skill being tested in relation to each question into an excel grid. When you add the pupil names use alphabetical order. As you mark, digitally record their quantitative result for each question. The analysis will be well worth the effort as it will give you a picture of areas of weakness for the individual children - as well as the whole cohort - which is particularly useful when deciding on remedial strategies and planning effective lessons. When this is complete, print it out and at a glance, you will be able to see which areas you need to plan for as a priority and you won't need to waste time on areas where the majority of pupils understood. Write them down and place them in your in-tray. If there are only a handful of students who didn't grasp a concept, write their names on a post-it and place it in your in-tray. Later, when it comes to processing, you can decide how you will plan these into your lesson, or you may even address a misconception there and then.

Formative Feedback

Unlike summative feedback, formative feedback is designed to lead directly to our desired objective - i.e. helping our student to learn faster. With formative feedback, the majority of time should be spent in reviewing the work but the actual giving of the feedback should happen at the earliest opportunity. Ideally, such feedback should be delivered verbally to each student relative to need. However, a busy teaching environment presents challenges for the teacher to provide considered and timely feedback. Verbal feedback can be general in nature (i.e. directed to the whole class) but this means it is not private. It can be specific but this will be limited to the teacher's capacity to identify needs as they arise during the course of the lesson. It is likely that even the most practised teacher will occasionally miss the pupil who quietly didn't understand or one who appeared not to but clearly did. Verbal feedback also has the drawback of being an unavoidably public affair, which means it may negatively affect pupils' self-esteem presenting a potential barrier to learning. All realities considered, the kind of quality feedback pupils need to achieve will not be possible within the context of the lesson alone. Setting up one-to-one appointments for students whilst other students concentrate on a self-directed task is a fantastic way to provide detailed and personalised feedback. However, such practice doesn't allow for the degree of general teacher input required for a regular lesson so cannot become the default option for providing formative feedback. This is why formative feedback traditionally occurs as a written comment on the students' work. Written feedback enables the teacher to distribute his/ her attention proportionately using the peace and quiet between lessons to enable them to focus and carefully examine the work.

However this practice can be labour intensive and you need to ensure that the time cost is relative to the pupil progress which will result from it. It is possible to combine the speed of verbal feedback with benefits of the written word if you use software to dictate your feedback and then have it printed out as a sticker. Dictation software typically promises to enable you to mark 'a piece of work a minute' which means (in theory), you can mark a class-worth of work half an hour. When a teacher at my school was diagnosed with carpel tunnel syndrome -which makes writing a strain - we had the software paid for as part of her occupational health arrangement. However, within weeks, as soon as the symptoms had eased, I noticed she had abandoned using the software and the printer lay dormant on her desk. Interestingly the reason she gave for no longer using the software was that she had ran out of the special printer roll required to print the stickers. Yet she wouldn't allow her car to run out of petrol and simply walk to and from school, so why was this situation different. One possible answer points to a fundamental characteristic of human nature. At the time of writing, this type of software is embryonic, which means that it requires a great deal of trouble-shooting to use it effectively. There are also very few people using it, so help is not readily available when it is required. If a ritual is not easy to perform, it is very unlikely to become a habit. This is due to a simple fact which tends to be either forgotten or denied the majority of the time. It is the main reason that plans rarely materialise and that success is uncommon: humans will *always* default to the easiest option. The only reason we can overcome immediate hardship for future gains is because we have been able to temporality do so enough to create a habit. Once something becomes a habit, it is easier to follow through with the action then not and this is what causes the tipping point. The amount of days required to turn a behaviour into a habit is different depending on who you talk to but however long it takes. However, what you can know for sure is that if you never get to reach the tipping point, the behaviour won't ever become a habit. Therefore it will always be easier *not* to do it than to do it. The teacher in this case had not given the behaviour enough of a chance to embed before she stopped and defaulted to her old ways.

With this in mind, the teacher should establish a procedure which allows formative assessment to happen as naturally and fluidly as possible and then repeat it until it embeds. As we discussed in Principle Seven, using time and place associations can help you to get into the correct channel which will maximise efficiency. Just as you might leave your running shoes by the front door if you intend to go for a run, take as many barriers as you can out of the way. In keeping with the batching principle, you need to ensure un-marked work has its own space in which it can be stored and a protected timeslot in which it will become your number one priority. Just like any skill, if you practise your marking at regular protected times, the law of incremental gains means you will improve, making the process more manageable. You may work in a school which prescribes a particular kind of marking process or you may work in a school with a more relaxed policy. Whatever your policy states, it is important that you maintain ownership of your practice. Always keep the reason you provide feedback at the forefront of your mind. Rather than getting caught up with the idea that feedback should look a certain way, it can be helpful to think of written feedback as forming part of a hierarchy rather than a simple binary decision to mark or not mark. With each step at the hierarchy, feedback will have a deeper impact on the progress of the student. We should endeavour at the very least, to ensure that a very basic level

161

of feedback takes place for every piece of work.

Hierarchy of Formative Feedback

Self-reflection: the first stage of feedback comes from the person responsible for the action. In a marking context, this involves the pupil checking his or her own work and the teacher encouraging them to do so. This saves you time because your subsequent marking is more meaningful as it will pick up on improvements that the student him or herself would not have identified rather than those he or she could have identified on their own. When you point out errors that the student could have identified for himself, the sense of frustration can cause him to dismiss your marking and this prevents learning from taking place.

Establish a Logical System

As with summative assessment, once pupils have looked at their own work, ensure all work is open at the page you intend to mark. As mentioned earlier, it is good practice to establish the classroom habit of pupils submitting work in register order. Keeping the learning intention in mind, scan for high competency, medium competency and low competency work focussing on this outcome. Essentially, whether pupils 'got it', 'didn't get it' or 'partially got it' and classify the work into three piles using this criteria.

Identify the Successes

Beginning with the high competency work, look at the first piece of work carefully, making corrections to the body of the work and writing a brief positive comment below it, identifying which skill or understanding the pupil has successfully demonstrated. You can follow your own school policy here, identifying 'what worked well' for example. You will likely find that the previous step has enabled you to essentially repeat the same comment or code a number of times. Use the first book as a template for all the other work of similar quality and simply repeat the process for the other two piles. Of course the exact comments may not be appropriate for all books but if you had a good scan to begin with, you will be surprised how many comments *are* relevant. Handwriting will double in speed if you ensure you are literally repeating the same comment word for word each time.

Identify Next Steps

Finally, repeat the process with a direction for improvement. This step is the most important step in the learning process and should move them along in some way. In some schools a marking key is used where a number or code relates to a next action such as 'check your spellings'. This can make the process even quicker but requires initial pupil training to get them used to the meaning of the codes. One example of good practice is to ask a question designed to stretch, challenge or intrigue your pupil and below it draw a highlighted box (the correct size for the length of the expected response).

Pupil Response

If you are concerned that after hours of marking pupils won't even look at your comments, let alone read and respond to them, first ask why the child is not responding to the comments so you can address the real problem. Unfortunately, traditional methods have trained pupils to be passive recipients of learning and it takes a persistent teacher to reverse this habit. First and foremost, you should expect a response, just as you would to a verbal comment. Scaffold suitable responses just as you would your written comments. Some ways to train your pupils to respond appropriately to comments are:

1. Draw a little highlighted box below a comment that requires a written response;

2. Embed rewards into your comments such as merits or house points to encourage careful review of the comment;

3. Where appropriate, write comments which show you have appreciated the work on its own merit such as 'really?' Or 'me too';

4. Verbally reinforce comments whilst the student is beside you and check they understand what to do next;

5. At times it may be appropriate to respond to the response to encourage further review of the work.

As well as training, students will need a dedicated time to respond to feedback. Often referred to by the playful acronym DIRT (Directed Improvement and Response Time), the idea is that pupils are allocated time to read and respond to the comments on their work. Students who are expected to respond to feedback and given the chance to do so will come to view learning as a two-way process, which is a pivotal step in progression. When you provide an opportunity for the students to respond to your feedback, this also has the happy side-effect of closing the habit loop for yourself. You receive the reward of knowing that your feedback has had an impact, meaning that in the future, you are more likely to want to mark as soon as possible after the work is completed.

An External Audience

The most powerful form of feedback is to give the work an external audience. This provides further motivation for the learner to review the work to ensure it is up to standard and gives the work a purpose. Whilst the student prepares her work for publishing, she will be internally motivated to further edit, seeking to leave the best possible impression of her capability. If the audience is always the same, the effect is reduced, so it is important to make it as varied as possible. Take opportunity to showcase the work to peers through the use of a visualizer; visitors; senior members of staff or parents.

Feedback is one of the crucial elements of the triangle of teacher purpose: planning, teaching, feedback. If you try to save time by cutting out one of the fundamental aspects of your job – you will find that you are not effectively doing your job. For students to make progress, they need to produce better work each lesson. In order for this to happen, you need to get them in the habit of producing excellent work and improving this each lesson. As we have seen, effective feedback can achieve this by operating on a number of levels, providing the student with:

- A quality-check: ensuring the work is accurate
- Advice: giving strategies for improvement
- Acknowledgement: acknowledging the meaning of the work
- Reinforcement: rewarding the behaviour of improving work
- A memorable record: allowing for future reference

Whilst it is these ends in themselves which count, rather than the manner in which they are achieved, formative written feedback is often the most efficient medium we can use. However, marking, like all forms of feedback, should be undertaken to stimulate a commensurate level of progress. It is crucial that we mark smart, spending the time in the areas which matter, and feed into our essential purpose of facilitating pupil progress and efficiently automatizing all other parts of the process

PRINICIPLE NINE

TEACH YOUR PUPILS TO THINK FOR THEMSELVES

'You can't learn in school what the world is going to do next year.'

- Henry Ford

The biggest time-waster of any leadership role is poor delegation. Effective people have learned to manage each step towards every outcome often. Rather understandably, they often come to believe that this is the best way to ensure positive outcomes for those whom they lead. In business, we call this approach 'micro-managing'. It has a bad reputation for facilitating the kind of learned helplessness for which the manager only has themselves to blame. In education we call this *teaching*.

You might have experienced a great deal of comfort, satisfaction and most likely success from breaking down objectives into tasks and these into so-called 'Steps for Success'. However, whilst it might feel like your job, it is not. Your job is to teach students to visualise their own goals, learn from mistakes and to cultivate an internal locus of control which will draw them away from your apron strings and out into the real world. It is time to get to grips with the uncomfortable reality: giving pupils trust and independence is the only way they will be able to meet their full potential. Your purpose as a teacher is to facilitate a fundamental willingness to learn not to micromanage a particular output. Whatever the output turns out to be, it will be far greater and more meaningful when it is driven by the self-motivated pupil. The key is in making sure they understand how learning works so you can teach them to use it and then step aside. Thankfully this approach has a very pleasing side effect: it will save you a whole lot of wasted time!

I understand first-hand the kind of mind shift this requires. I achieved very good results from breaking down tasks using Steps for Success; it has always been my default method and is not inherently bad. However an over-reliance on this approach has significant implications for the learner. A useful way to think about this is when you consider how you learnt to ride a bike. When I grew up, it was common to use these little trainer wheels. They did nothing to help you learn but did enable you to ride the bike. However, when you took them off, often when you were six or so, you had to go through the whole process of learning from scratch, only this time it was made more difficult because you were used to having the trainer wheels and had come to rely upon them. Nowadays it is common to use the 'balance bike' approach: that is giving a child a bike with two wheels and no pedals to start with. My son was given a balance bike as soon as he could walk. He had just turned two when he learned to ride his first push bike. He didn't so much learn as simply get on it and ride. This story points to something fundamental about the nature of learning: a child is born inquisitive and does not need to be taught how to learn. A needless problem arises when we give them training wheels anyway. When we finally take the wheels off, often as late as age eighteen, the child feels foolish and wobbly. Sadly, the reaction is often to convince himself that he probably doesn't need to learn to ride a bike anyway. By then, the fear of falling built by so many years of relying on the training wheels is both out of proportion and deeply engrained. The learner, both literally and metaphorically, has much further to fall.

As teachers we tend to over-structure learning, imposing our own boundaries on how problems are to be solved, and breaking down solutions into simple steps.

We are held accountable to meet particular learning outcomes but it does not necessarily follow that we train the pupils to meet those outcomes in exactly the same way we would approach them, especially not with the same levels of fear! This is not because the teachers don't really want to give their pupils more independence but that they are unable to transcend their own fear in order to let this happen. The fear is that when given the chance, children will choose what is easy rather than what is challenging. They will choose to do the things they enjoy rather than the things that they need to learn to pass exams. However, we mustn't forget that we all do things we don't want to do without coercion or force from anyone but ourselves. We only do this when we are confident that it will lead to outcomes we want. We have learnt delayed gratification because most when we broke free from the training wheels, we felt the consequences for ourselves. Well-adjusted young people will bounce back one or two times before consciously re-establishing the good habit for themselves whilst less well-adjusted people may continue bouncing for longer. Some of us may grow up in a household where these good habits were never instilled in us to begin with and we may have to learn the hard way right from the very beginning. In any case, we all must learn the skill at some point and we are capable of learning it much earlier than you may think. The crucial trigger for learning the benefits of delayed gratification is the experience of making the *wrong* choice and the opportunity to take responsibility for that choice. Conclusive failure comes not from the choice but from offering the choice without the accompanying responsibility for the outcome. Pupils should be aware that they are always given choices and that your role is to guide them in these choices. You explain and present the choices, linking the choice to the expected outcome; but it should always be a genuine choice.

Genuine choice always allows the opportunity to

choose not to work at all. However, as the teacher, this shouldn't be something you fear. If pupils choose not to work, then you should choose not to help them complete the work. It is in facilitating the choice to learn that is the purpose of your job *not* in getting the work done! Intervene only when the pupil's negative choices cause a distraction or highjack your attention. Make it clear that the teacher and teaching assistant attention is there only for their safety and their right to learn. This will make the path of least resistance to work. Yet this scenario is alarmingly common: a passive student waits around for the hardworking teacher or teaching assistant to tell them what to do next, even to the point of equipping them with stationery. This state of affairs will gradually erode the pupil's imitative and they begin to embody a comfortable state of learned helplessness. When the pupil gets to the stage where they ask for guidance to meet the required outcome, support can be given but not without first encouraging the pupils to draw on their own resources. You should give students strategies for when they get stuck to help them build resilience. Try the '3 B4 me' approach where students are expected to try to find the answer using three different strategies before defaulting to the teacher. I encourage students to:

- Ask yourself
- Ask a friend
- Ask a text
- Ask a teacher

Encourage your students to look first in their own mind for the answer or to refer back to their own notes, then to ask a friend. If the answer cannot be found, they can consult a secondary resource such as a book or the internet and finally, if they fail to find the answer through these means they can ask an adult for help accessing these sources. A fun alliterative name for this strategy is the 'Brain, Book, Buddy and Boss' approach. You could also try a ticketing system like the one they use in Argos. Whilst they are waiting for their number to be called, the students have the chance to try trouble-shooting the problem using other strategies.

Another understandable fear regarding this hands-off approach is that pupils will choose something too ambitious and will get all their work 'wrong'. I know how it feels to peek at the work through a squinted eye you daren't face a page full of work that is partly or entirely incorrect. You feel as though there are so many next steps and feel guilty there is not anything positive to say. Again, it is essential that we keep our eye on what is important. In this case, there is plenty of progress to be made and that is good news for a teacher. Next steps always trump identifying what went well. If the work appears perfect and without mistake and you can't reasonably fathom what the student needs to do to progress to the next level - *this* is a cause for concern. If the work was too easy for the pupil, as far as your purpose is concerned, the activity was nothing short of pointless. Besides, the very fact that the student has chosen to take on the challenge is cause for genuine praise: they have taken a necessary risk that many would not brave. Errors in a pupil's work should be celebrated as these confirm two things: the work was not too easy; you did not give them too much help. During the time I began teaching it was very fashionable to leave mistakes uncorrected for fear of damaging the pupil's self-esteem. In fact, despite recent curriculum reform to a system which demands rote learning of a specific body of facts and leaves no room for even the smallest error, in some pockets of education, this fear of critiquing pupil's work still persists and is stubbornly defended by teachers and heads alike.

If you don't teach students not only to accept but to

welcome criticism, you are missing the purpose of teaching. Mistakes are at the heart of the learning which it is your purpose to facilitate but you can only learn new things in one of two ways: from our own mistakes or from those of others. So get your students out there and coach them to try things and to make mistakes. They need to understand that if they are not making mistakes that they are not learning and it is not possible for them to progress. Encourage collaboration, reward 'out of the box' thinking and students who share their mistakes. Try giving expected outcomes rather than 'steps for success' and take a step back. The longer the training wheels have been on, the longer it will usually take for the students to flourish but hold your nerve and be patient. When the scores a low test result: don't panic. Tell them it is a perfectly normal part of the learning process and let them have another go. Popular tools such as James Nottingham's 'Learning Pit' and Carol Dweck's 'Growth Mind-set' brain can be really useful to normalise this sort of thinking in a classroom.

In case you are unfamiliar with these tools, James Nottingham designed the 'learning pit' as a model to demonstrate how learning takes place. It is common to think of learning as a vertical progression from simple to the abstract or simply the cumulative acquisition of knowledge from a little to a lot as one grows and learns. The learning pit is a way to demonstrate what *really* happens between the stages of learning and serves to explain why many people plateau at a certain level rather than steadily progressing to the next stage. If learning happened without feedback, then everyone would continue to progress steadily throughout their lives. Learning will progress to a certain point until what we already know doesn't suffice to move us to the next level. James Nottingham uses the analogy of the 'learning pit' to demonstrate how we feel when we come across a problem

173

like this and need to figure out a way to overcome it. It is important that learners recognise this feeling as a necessary part of the learning process, or they will experience it like the world is against them. All learners have felt that at some point: as though they have something wrong with them which means they can't achieve a particular objective. When someone encourages them to go for it, they will nod their head whilst thinking in the back of their mind, *They make that sound so easy; I bet that's because it's easy for them but they don't really get how especially difficult that would be for me.* But until they realise it's hard for everyone, it is possible for people to stay in the 'pit' for most of their lives; that is unless they climb back up to where they were before they began. The irony is, it takes almost as much energy to avoid the pit as it would to go through it and yet the only reward is staying the same. That is how many people live their lives, either avoiding the important pits or persuading others to carry them across. Even when they get pushed in by a well-meaning friend or teacher, they wear themselves out clawing back up the side they came in. James Nottingham's pit points to why feedback is crucial. The 'pickier' the feedback, the more the learner will get used to a situation where there is always a way to improve what has been done before. Rather than that rather sticky habit many of us fall into where we move from one situation to another similar situation repeating the same mistakes each time. According to Ray Dalio, when we get experienced in life, we will come to realise that it is merely a sequence of situations we have already come across. He calls them 'just another one of those'. We must learn that each time we encounter 'another one of those', the aim is to do better than the last time we encountered it by repeating on the strengths and focussing on the weaknesses. Dweck's concept of 'growth mind-set' is based on the very same principle, encouraging learners to get comfortable with feeling uncomfortable. Those students who despair at mistakes, immediately retreating to easier work when they occur have what is called a 'fixed mind-set'. To these students, intelligence is fixed and people reach a pre-destined peak beyond which they are unable to progress. They use this idea to explain why tricky work feels hard: they believe it is literally impossible - for them. Conversely, those students with a growth mind-set understand that making mistakes is a natural part of the learning process. When they find something difficult, they believe they are unable to do it at present but will one day, with enough practice be able to get there. Carol Dweck argues we are in danger of reinforcing a fixed mind-set in schools with our ingrained habit of praising correct answers rather than the mistakes which indicate learning is taking place.

Dweck argues that if we want students to learn to accept their mistakes gracefully, we need to consider the way we praise them. Students are trained to check before they act, to listen carefully to instructions and to finish their tasks. It is easy to see why teachers may praise the behaviours as described above and they are born out of a desire to manage the pupils' behaviour and to minimise disruption. However in order to promote independence we should praise initiative rather than conformity. We are fostering a culture of excessive checking, over-reliance on particular models for completing tasks and an unhealthy obsession with 'finishing' tasks such as worksheets which overshadows the purpose of learning. In short, we are creating passive learners. Instead, teachers should encourage pupils to share with us their unique solutions rather than to give us their problems. The pupils need to come to believe that the best solutions will come from them. The best way to do this is to stop providing fully formed solutions but to reframe your response as a question which will encourage them to look within. If you throw the stick, the dog will only keep coming back with it. Teaching your students to learn for themselves creates more of impact than you could ever have by telling them a tried and tested process first hand.

As teachers, we tend to assume it is our job to make sure the children are learning at the appropriate level for them when actually this should be the responsibility of the learner. When we allow students to choose their own task, you are giving them access to autonomy: one of the prerequisites for internal motivation. Furthermore, the student who chooses their own task reveals something of interest to the teacher about their learning style. Outliers who either choose a task which is too easy or one which is too difficult suffer with a misunderstanding about what learning is all about. The first student has learnt about the power of completion as discussed in Principle Two and confuses this with learning. He has a fixed mind-set. You need to support this child with his mode of thinking by 'throwing him in the pit' with a challenging conversation. The second child most likely has a growth mind-set and has probably been under attaining for far too long without access to the challenging work he really wants to complete. He will need plenty of targeted guidance from you to help them to attain his aspirational goal.

Establishing the correct learning behaviour will not happen if you take off the trainer-wheels and allow the student to crash. Instead, you can guide students in this direction gradually, taking steps forward and back if need be. You want to reach a point where your need to 'manage' the behaviour becomes something invisible to an observer. The management of learning behaviour should appear on a scale of progression with three 'levels', where the first step the power is in the hands of the teacher and the final step places the power over to the pupil.

THE HIERACHY OF LEARNING BEHAVIOUR

Level One

The first level represents a dictatorial culture is embodied by the use of direct instruction in the form of imperative statements which may or may not have a polite tag at the end e.g. *Finish that question* (please). The power is largely in the hands of the teacher.

Level Two

The second level represents a democratic culture and is embodied by the polite request: this will not begin with the imperative phrase and may come in the form of a rhetorical question. Both the speaker and the listener should understand that an action is required. E.g. *could you please finish that question?* In this situation, the power balanced between student and teacher.

Level Three

The third level represents a liberal culture is embodied by reflective questioning: this is questioning designed to ask the listener to think or reflect. It often asks the listener to consider something: *Do you think you could finish that question?* He could say no and would have no fear of being defiant. But it forces him to think. Does he *want* to say no? In this scenario, the power is in the hands of the student.

In this third level, you should always place the onus back upon the student. This entails acting in such a way that forces them to reflect on whether their behaviour will help them to meet their own intentions. The more you pass these types of comments to the student, the more reflective they will become. Finally the behaviour needs to be reinforced with trust. You allow the student to complete tasks of his or her own choosing, asking only to see them when complete. If the task is not up to standard, resist the urge to regress immediately back to stage one. Instead ask them a 'stage three' focussing question.

"Did you find it hard to complete this?" "Did you try your best on this?" "Do you want me to help you with this?"

Giving instructions will always take time, but if your pupils remain at the stage where they require stage one instructions to complete tasks, not only will it take far more time than necessary but it will be time ill-used from the perspective of your purpose. You know as well as I do that 'stage one' instructions (steps for success style) will get the work done and keep behaviour in check. Unfortunately, the effect is limited to when you are physically present and you need to be entirely focussed on giving the instructions. Which begs the question of what happens when you are not. Whilst there is merit in all forms of instruction, it is important from a time-economy perspective that you use as few 'stage one' type questions as you can manage. These are time consuming and largely unnecessary. Save the stage-ones for pre-schoolers in the autumn term, hazardous situations or written instructions on the board designed to keep students quiet! One important thing you should bear in mind is if you decide it is appropriate to give 'stage one' instructions, always write them down to avoid having to repeat them.

As well as guiding the students to choose their own learning challenges, they need to be taught to see the bigger picture and be focussed on their future goals. Future focus will help them to become more purposeful and will be more successful. Asking them to set their own goals can be tricky, particularly if you have very young students, but it is necessary. If students are not able to visualise their goals, they will not be able to achieve them. A great place to start is asking them to write about or discuss their future life. When you put them into that mind-set, they have to acknowledge what they want, even if it's just a possibility and it puts them in the wavelength of achieving it. It is a task that can be linked to any subject-e.g. Science: what science will you use in the future and how will it enrich your life? Modern Languages: Can you think of how your language skills will help you to achieve your goals? History: What contribution will you make towards future history books? It is even more powerful if they imagine the future as if it is happening right now. Another assignment to set might be to write an exam transcript, making it look as realistic as possible using the pupils' aspirational grades or asking the students to write letters to their future selves or their end of term reports.

By expecting pro-activity and encouraging a growth mind-set, students will come to see themselves as having the power to shape the world around them rather than looking to you for answers. If you can successfully teach them how to learn, the students in your classes will learn to use their initiative when troubles arise, and will trouble-shoot issues for themselves and their peers. This will enable you to step out of the equation and become a facilitator, 'guide on the side' and finally a passive observer. The ultimate aim is to preserve your time, energy and focus for the things that will make the most impact on your purpose: facilitating learning. Spend your time, energy and focus on coaching your pupils to overcome their motivation barriers. Find out what drives them and what is getting in the way. Your will-power and that of your students is limited, therefore you want to avoid wasting it on cajoling unwilling recipients. Compared with the micromanager approach, this is time and energy consuming but the difference between the two is that time, energy and focus spent on your actual priority, rather than a pseudo-priority like 'getting work done' or 'managing their behaviour'. The more on purpose your students are, the less wasted time and energy you will waste keeping them going in the right direction. Before long, your initial time-investment will be repaid as when you work on purpose, you make progress. Ultimately, the key to ensure you are working on purpose is to ensure your pupils are working on purpose.

PRINCIPLE TEN

MAKE EACH MINUTE COUNT

'It has been my observation that most people get ahead during the time that others waste.'

- Henry Ford

Now you have a clear idea of your purpose: to facilitate learning and the priority tasks which will enable you to achieve this: planning and preparation, teaching and feedback, it is time to consider how you will extricate yourself from the multitude of remaining tasks and interruptions so you can get on with these. The first step to avoid wasting your time is to recognise the biggest time-thieves for what (and who) they are. Time-thieves steal your precious minutes and give very little (if anything) back. One of the top offenders is unnecessary 'processing'.

Manage Unnecessary Processing

As mentioned in Principe Two, 'Processing' refers to the act of deciding what to do about something and when to do it. To compound its affects, every decision you make uses the energy twice, as it becomes a decision not to do something else. You may not be aware of how much of your mental energy and time is given over to processing because it occurs as an automatically. Even in a world without the stimulus of social media, it will occur hundreds of times a day and demand your valuable attention and energy. In addition to the more obvious circumstances such as sorting through emails, processing can happen unconsciously every time a new decision needs to be made:

watch or don't watch, pay or don't pay, call or don't call. These decisions can feel like unavoidable aspects of everyday life but it is possible to take control of them. The trick is to make processing intentional and to batch it as with any other task to make it is efficient as possible.

If you followed the advice in Principle Two, you now have a physical in tray and one in your email account. The trick is to process these trays at set times each day; reduce them to zero and then leave them alone until the next scheduled slot. Checking your email first thing in the morning is a productivity faux par. If this is the first time you have heard this advice, the reason is: if you begin with your in-box, you are starting your day with other people's priorities. This is not a good start and the effects will stay with you for the rest of the day. We discussed in Principle Five how the morning is the time where others are most likely to be absent or leave you alone. Furthermore, having been at your longest period of rest, your energy reserves are likely to be at their peak which has the effect of multiplying your time. You should use this time to complete your most important tasks. Now before your pupils are in school, it is of course not possible to teach your pupils, but if you have any influence over your teaching timetable, you will be aware that pupils are most engaged first thing in the morning and are therefore more receptive to lessons. This is the Perato Principle in action again: twenty percent of your input leads to eighty percent of results. Make sure the input is on your most important work. So of course in the morning, prior to the students arriving, spend this crucial time not on processing but on producing key results: either planning or marking.

Processing can be done in less valuable time slots, for example at break time or lunch time. However, make sure you follow the guidance in Principle Two and only process during this time: that is decide what when where about the particular item and then move on to the next. This goes for email as well as your physical inbox items. It is important that you set yourself clear boundaries. If you find yourself processing at an unscheduled time, stop. In no uncertain terms, you are opening a can of worms and needlessly throwing away your mental energy. If you want to multiply your time, you will need to develop a bias for action. That means you want to spend most of your time, especially your high-energy time: *acting*. You must be absolutely clear that whilst processing keeps you busy and tends to fill your days, it is **not** action. It is the necessary precursor to action. Processing is to action is like cooking is to dining or practice to performance. It can make you feel productive; it can even be very enjoyable in itself, however, it uses energy and if it does not lead to the necessary outcome, it is wholly inefficient, if not bordering on pointless. Reduce the time you spend on processing, particularly menial tasks and spend the time you save on your priorities.

Reduce Entertainment Media

Hopefully by now, when you are dealing with your in-trays, you are aware that you are processing. However, as mentioned earlier, engaging with entertainment media is also a form of processing, as it constantly demands that you make decisions about what you are experiencing. Either click or don't click, watch or don't watch, buy or don't buy, subscribe or don't subscribe. This is no accident: it is designed this way. Unless you belong to a particular religious community which prohibits use of such frivolities, entertainment media such as newspapers, television and radio have most likely been part of your life since birth. It is also likely that you engage - at least to some extent - with social media.

As is probably clear to you by now, I have a reverent respect for technology and its potential to expand your mind. You may have noticed the references to Henry

Ford throughout and my various suggestions to adapt to digital systems. However, I like many others in my generation, am suitably suspicious of entertainment media. Since the dawn of time, people who have grown up without certain technological advances have been suspicious of their effects and I am a stark example of this rule. When I was thirteen, a visitor to our school came to talk about time management and she said one thing that always stuck in my mind. 'Switch off the television when you have finished watching it.' I had grown up in one of those households where the television is always on in the background, even if no-one's watching it. Interestingly this was not because it was the culture of my family as one might assume but because I was a latch-key child and spend plenty of time alone. So naturally, I turned on the television - 'for company' at first, and then out of habit. It wasn't the profundity of the visiting speaker's suggestion which stuck with me; it was obvious to say the least. What struck me was the difficulty I experienced in trying to carry it out. It took me several failed attempts over the course of that week to do as she had suggested. When I finally achieved it and I knew I had control, I would find myself spending long periods staring at the dormant TV set. It was a large, wooden monstrosity in those days. I would stare at my silent adversary and wonder how it had control of me. Thanks to that moment when I gave the idea proper consideration, I have always held entertainment media at arms-length. I have explored it but pulled away regularly to reassure myself that I am in control. Now I know about the power of habit loops and how the makers of digital media take full advantage of the 'trigger-behaviour-reward cycle' to keep you hooked. But society is just beginning to wake up to the damage that social media is causing and perhaps 'digital dementia' and addiction are only the tip of the ice-burg. Even of the most sheltered students will face mental and social challenges that we did not and develop and diminish academic abilities which are different to our own and the result of the society in which we live.

Not to labour the point, but all forms of entertainment media now actively utilise the psychology of to keep us in addicted. The glossy magazines, the news the click-bait news articles, the pop-up adverts on all digital devices which eerily seem to know exactly what we happened to want to buy or know are carefully engineered to utilise the power of the habit to keep you hooked. They shamelessly use triggers to attract your attention. Once they have it, they issue a reward in the hope that you continue with the behaviour.

Even if you don't feel entertainment is harmful, you cannot deny it is a time-consumer. Only you can judge whether what it gives you in return is equal to your precious minutes.

Avoid Switch-Tasking

Switch-tasking, as we discussed in Principle One, happens when you attempt to complete two tasks at the same time. As you will know by now, the reality is you are not completing either task to your best ability and you are spending more time completing each task than you would if you were to complete them separately. This is due to the time lost as you switch and have to refocus on each task. Think of it as though you were attempting to photograph objects in the foreground and background at the same time. Imagine you had to take ten photographs of each. It wouldn't make sense to constantly re-adjust the lens between your photographs. It would obviously be quicker to adjust the lens once for the foreground and take the necessary photographs and then adjust the lens again for the background and take your ten photographs. However, people don't consider the need to refocus because it happens automatically. It may seem 'automatic' but is quite a complicated process, involving a change of mind-set and processing skills which initially would have taken a significant time to master. Automatic or not, refocussing when you change task takes time which needs to be factored in.

Make the Most of Waiting

If you are one of those people who is always early, you will have come to accept two things:

- Waiting is a fact of life
- People who are late are selfish and annoying

As it happens, I used to be one of those infuriating people who was always late. It was a bad habit which had me trapped me in a loop for many years. The only way to break the loop seemed to be to drastically overcompensate, getting ready much earlier than necessary, and even then I could never manage early: on time was the best I could do. These 'early' people eluded me - what special equipment did they have that I was missing? What puzzled me further was why this simple thing did not respond to the application of will-power, like so many other things in my life. I did not know about habits then. As we discussed earlier, habits lurk in all our daily actions and are disguised as decisions. What they really are is crude tryptic cycles beginning with a trigger, leading to an action and finalising with a reward. Like all habits, my late habit loop had these three elements but only the lateness part was evident. I finally solved this conundrum in counselling. It turns out that the late habit can be caused by the same triggers and rewards as the early habit: fear. If you are a person who is always early, you may harbour a fear of being late and the embarrassment or other consequences that may result from this. As you have rarely (or perhaps) never experienced this, your fear of the feeling is probably much greater than the actual feeling you might experience. However, for a late person, this fear is greatly reduced due to over-exposure. You realise the world doesn't end when you are late, and people largely expect lateness from at least one person. I discovered the hidden 'reward' for always being late was never needing to wait. Being late kept me always entering a situation at the height of action and then moving to the next in the same state. The fear of the quietness when intense focus subsides as one activity ends and preparation for the next begins kept me perpetually leaving at the last minute, so that the journey to the next event was intense and focussed, and this intense focus continued on arrival. Many hours of counselling later, my journey of self-discovery lead me to the reason I was afraid of being on time: it came from a fear of being alone with my thoughts. At this point, I knew I had to deal with the anxiety-inducing thoughts. Something I knew would take yet more hours of counselling. Thankfully, there was a much quicker short-term fix. My therapist suggested bringing with me a sort of portable in-tray of items to work on whilst I was waiting for things to begin. At the time this consisted of my normal work bag with a folder inside with some to-do items, some pens, a sharp pencil, a laptop, a book or other reading material and a highlighter. I would leave in good time, the journey filled with thoughts about what I would do with my 'bonus minutes' and then be all set to begin tasks once I arrived. I found that without the background stress of getting ready to leave, I was more productive during the waiting time than the time before I left. The habit was reset overnight and my journey towards making each minute count had begun. I can now fill any waking minute, either standing up or sitting down and my portable in-tray is now reduced to my mobile phone.

Whether you are afraid of your thoughts or not, waiting

is not a fact of life, unless you accept it as one. You can be productive wherever you are and don't need to schedule huge blocks of 'dead' time either side of an appointment. If travel is necessary, make the necessary arrangements at the most time-efficient time (this usually isn't the time when everyone else is making their way to said destination) and then use the remaining time to complete a pre-arranged task. I must emphasise that the task you choose to complete should have already been through processing and you should know exactly what you want to achieve as an outcome before you arrive at the destination. You should also consider a secluded spot to bed down in. If you are waiting, you are particularly vulnerable to interruptions because others view your time as 'dead' time. If you in any way look as though you are in transition you will become a target. Get in, focus and complete your task with as little fuss as possible.

Reducing Repetition

Call me intolerant but I personally find repeating oneself to be not only a highly inefficient way for one to spend their time but it is also prodigiously irritating. We teachers have come to accept at least some repetition as not only a normal part of their practice but a necessary part of the learning cycle. Repetition is the staple diet of pupils following old-school instruction, repeating facts which must be memorised regularly in the hope that they will eventually sink in. For many it is abhorrent to hear the chant of pupils reciting times tables or observe pupils conducting drill. The assumption is that rote-learning facts creates a culture of mindless subordination and destroys pupils' ability to think critically. There is, of course, merit to this assumption in that habit-formation is a proven technique for retaining information and it remains the underlying tenet of the 'cyclical curriculum' whereby key

189

subjects are revisited each year in the hope that each time the subject is covered, one will be able to do so in more depth than the last. Whilst this curricular structure is beginning to give way to a 'mastery' curriculum (whereby subjects are studied for much longer periods to enable pupils to be immersed in the subject and to explore and apply it in many different ways before moving on to another) it still forms the backbone of the modern curriculum. Indeed, whilst the mastery curriculum does not require structural repetition, it relies fundamentally on a body of core facts which must be deeply embedded in the pupils' mind prior to application. However, despite the fact that the curriculum relies upon students retaining facts, the requirement for repetition can be reduced greatly by making some subtle yet crucial changes to your practice. To reduce repetition, you will need to make the material as memorable as possible. That way, all you will need is a trigger and the pupil will be able to easily recall the information. Here are two simple techniques that can be used for any type of information and don't require any type of special resources to make them possible:

- Teach new material using as many media as possible all at once
- Adapt the material to make it funny, clever, surprising or anecdotal

This will rouse the attention of the students and make them more receptive to future trigger memories, making over-learning more natural and alleviating the need for time-consuming repetition.

Another type of repetition you will commonly fall foul to, is the repetition of basic instructions. The most decisive way to alleviate this type of repetition is to do away with the need for students to perform tasks or behave in a very particular way, such as copying the learning objective in a certain format or the use of particular colour pen etc. Of course, it is unlikely that your schools policies will allow this. If this is the case, then unfortunately a certain level of 'training' will be required and it is the unavoidable fact the regular reinforcement required to achieve this will eat into your precious teaching time. My friend Alicia worked in a junior school with four forms sharing a single very tight cloak area. This meant that at the start and end of the school day and break times all four classes of pupils would be confined to a very small space. Two of the pupils within this space had ADHD and incidents were frequent. In order to manage the space safely, the pupils had to enter the space at scheduled times, which meant the whole operation took at least 15 minutes each time it was required. She calculated that the pupils were missing up to a full lesson each day simply retrieving and setting down their belongings. When Alicia asked her Headteacher if this situation could be resolved by simply separating the coat pegs into distinct areas, he responded by suggesting that she 'train' the children to behave appropriately whilst in the confined space instead. Anyone who has had the joy of teaching junior-age pupils can imagine how successful the cloakroom training endeavour was. The moral of the story is that if simple fundamental changes will save 'training' pupils to perform any otherwise unnecessary and mundane task, then this should be done as a first resort. It takes time and energy to provide training of any sort, so the skills we invest this in should at least be worthwhile to the pupil.

If training is required, try to be consistent enough in your instructions and expectations that your pupils will anticipate these without you having to verbalise them. Another way to embed instructions more deeply is to present them alongside a visual such as a simple written diagram or list. This will enable most students to go about their day with very few instructions given. However, there will still be some pupils who require the repetition much longer than others before they are confident enough not to require repetition. If you create the culture of the majority of pupils knowing 'how things are done', then this in itself will release you from having to do the repetition. The echo of your words will come from the students. With reference to the previous chapter, training through consistent repetition is the opposite of teaching the kids to think for themselves. You are, where 'training' is required, teaching the pupils to internalise your ready-made systems instead of encouraging them to develop their own. However, this is in itself a necessary skill and is therefore not inherently 'bad'. Teaching pupils to internalise processes quickly is also teaching them to learn what is fixed as well as what is fluid within a particular set of circumstances. Knowing when compliance is necessary and when you can negotiate, after all, is an essential skill in learning to think for yourself. You need to know with confidence where the box is before you can think outside it.

Manage Interruptions

In comparison to all the time thieves discussed above, interruptions incur the most significant cost by far. There are two reasons that interruptions have been allowed to become so prevalent in our in our lives. Firstly, it is because it is considered socially unacceptable to succumb to the annoyance they create. A good parent, leader or teacher is perceived as calm, approachable and 'available'. Secondly, they are to an extent a hidden time-consumer. People realise time is wasted but often profoundly underestimate impact of interruptions. Be particularly wary of those who argue 'but it will only take a minute' in surprise when you claim you do not have the time. Even if it does only take a minute, the time cost is always more. Tim Ferris (author of the 'Four Day Work Week') claims that on average, approximately 28 percent of the day is consumed by interruptions. For a teacher, this percentage is likely to seem much, much higher. Higher still for a teacher who is also a parent. Like switch-tasking, interruptions have a hidden cost as well as the obvious cost of time lost to respond to the interruption. Furthermore, if you are anticipating being interrupted, the energy and time it takes to refocus applies before the interruption as well as during and, as we shall see, after. If you want to claim your time back, it is important that you take control of this lethal time-consumer.

It is important first to distinguish between minimising distractions and minimising interruptions. A distraction is a passive occurrence and can mean different things to different people. For example, I can ignore the sound of a building site but get completely distracted by music with lyrics. I can't ignore clutter in my own home or office but can do so easily in another setting. This is because my mind doesn't perceive it as on offer to act, whereas music with lyrics tempts me to sing or listen to their meaning and my own mess calls me to tidy. You will likely try to minimise distractions as far as necessary for your level of tolerance. For a teacher, it is nigh-on impossible to create a sterile, blank environment in which to focus considering the majority of your time is spent in a classroom shared by others, only about 5 percent of which is under your immediate control. Therefore, I can safely assume you are not an easily-distracted person or the profession would have driven you to distraction long before you picked up this book. Having said this, I have the lower-end of tolerance levels. In my classroom, I manage distractions by ensuring the pupils are entirely focussed on the task at hand, whether they are working independently or in groups. For me, focussed noise is not a distraction whereas unfocussed noise is a call to attention. I like to keep my classroom orderly, and the pupils have been trained to be organised in the way they use it, with a place for everything and everything in its place. My colleagues have higher tolerance levels and the culture of their lessons is therefore different to mine.

In contrast, interruptions are interruptions, whoever you are. Having a high tolerance level to interruptions (i.e. being more open and approachable) will negatively affect your time more than if you have a lower tolerance. An interruption, as distinct from a distraction, doesn't just try to seduce you subtly in the background, like a flirtatious suitor fluttering their eyelashes from a distance. Whilst a distraction can be entertained (and enjoyed) or ignored at your digression. You can walk away from it freely if you choose. An interruption is a brash and demanding disruption outside of your control. Whilst it might come with an apology 'I'm sorry to interrupt' or something similar, an interruption by its very presence steals your attention without permission. Furthermore, an interruption makes you feel rude and uncomfortable if you choose not to engage with it. This switches your mind-set even more entirely from the subject at hand and forcing you to choose between navigating an uncomfortable social situation or focussing instead on what the interrupter wants for you to focus on and throwing the third option, getting on with the task *you* chose, out of the window entirely. Interruptions come in various forms, the most notoriously difficult to manage of which is the human interrupter.

The human interrupter is the most multi-faceted form of interruption. In addition to the straight forward cost of broken concentration and whatever new tasks it brings to your attention, there are a number of other factor to contend with. For example, the physical presence of the human interrupter can come with unexpected emotional pulls that steal your attention, sometimes for hours after the original interruption. Adolescent interrupters are of a very special sort. You may have come to accept this type of interruption as the norm. After having previously been baffled by this illogical perception, parenthood has enabled me to understand where this type of 'acceptance' comes from. It is a sort of resignation to deep-rooted guilt which states that you shouldn't be doing whatever you are doing whilst a child is present as they deserve your undivided attention simply by existing. However, for many parent or non-parent teachers with a higher degree of empathy than the author, this illogical yet very real affect applies adolescent interrupters of the student variety. Main thing to remember is that as much the child has the right to the attention of the adult, the adult equally has the right to use his attention to focus on what he or she sees as most important.

If you are to succeed in your battle with this type of interruption, you need to be long-sighted about your choice of action and you also take on each facet of the interruption separately. To summarise the main facets of a human interruption are as follows:

- The time lost to the interruption itself
- The subsequent break in concentration (this includes the time taken to refocus and regain momentum following the interruption)
- Time taken to process actions resulting from the interruption
- The distraction caused by residual emotional effects of the interruption

The cost of the human interruption can quickly rack up if you don't limit the damage by at least one of these facets, however I strongly advise you take action to prevent all of them by removing yourself physically from human distractions as far as you can. Of course for the teacher this affords precious little time but ring-fencing your PPA time and time before and after school will still be more productive than attempting to work at other times. The uninterrupted time - pound for pound - is worth far more. However, ring-fencing the time may be a challenge as you may find that the most common time for interruptions to take place *is* outside of teaching time. People seem to respect that you're busy during this time and therefore leave you to it. The interruptions you do get tend to be much shorter or even in a handwritten note format so that they don't require your immediate attention. These can go straight into your in-tray.

Kevin Kruse suggests training your co-workers to leave you alone by placing a 1440 on the front door of your work space (1440 relates to the number of minutes in the day in case you were wondering). If you are not in a leadership role, I would suggest that this is perhaps a little extreme. If you have this temperament I would perhaps suggest placing a sign which reads 'leave me alone'. It's less cryptic and therefore won't invite enquiries from curious interrupters. A less crude solution might be to simply close the door as often as possible. A closed door speaks volumes. You may find it difficult to close the door for this reason. If this is the case, you should remember that you cannot assume how others perceive it. Others may actually find it helpful to know when you don't mind being interrupted and when you do. If you pretend to be okay with being interrupted all the time, not only is it exhausting but it can be confusing for others who will clearly see through your façade when you become irritated. Failing the existence of a door, headphones can be a fantastic alternative. Make sure they are visible as they give the closed door message and also mean that objects in your periphery can be more easily ignored. Headphones are an invaluable part of my portable in-tray and I use larger ones for my stationary work areas. Whilst these physical signs will deter many, there will always be people who will knock at the closed door or even physically touch you to gain your attention. It is socially inappropriate to ignore these people and regardless of the resulting interruption, the knock itself has caused the break in flow. When such interruptions occur, you have no choice but to acknowledge them. However, the knockers and touchers are rare and usually operate out of convenience. If they can access you easily, they will do so. If they don't know where to find you, they won't. If you are accosted by the 'knocker', sometimes the best you can do is limit the time given to the interrupter by encouraging them to get to the point. "Hey I'm just in the middle of something, how can I help?" Is better than "Hi?" in answer to a knock at the door or a telephone. It is friendly but with a sense of urgency. Another technique for creating a sense of time sensitivity is to stand up, or even leave the room, taking the interrupter with you. What I've found works best is announcing to as many people as possible "right at x (start time) I'm going to hide myself away and try to really hammer out y (important task) prior to z (end time)". This makes the knocker, who tends to be less sensitive to subtle cues, explicitly aware that you are dealing with something important.

When an interruption occurs, it is important that you don't immediately put down a task. Try to ignore the interruption for long enough to come to a natural break in whatever you were doing. For example, if you are hearing a pupil read, make sure they come to the end of the sentence before asking if they wouldn't mind waiting a moment whilst the interruption takes place. If you were mid-sentence, finish it. If you were setting something down, takes moment to register where you set it down and to record the next action (either mentally or written). This will help you easily get back to your task following the interruption. This also has a subtle side-effect of letting the assailant know that he or she is interrupting, making them more conscious of the time they take from you. It is important that you get straight back on with your task as soon as they leave, making a note of any further action when they are still here and placing it in your in tray.

It is very likely that the interruption will entail further subsequent actions which will require processing. For example, the interrupter may request to borrow something, in which case the resultant action would be for you to find said item and pass it on. If the item is not to hand and will take longer to locate them the time it takes to write a note, it is important that you do not process the item at this time. Instead, write a reminder on the post-it and place the item into your in tray. A lot of the time, the interrupter will request an answer some sort. This can be very time-consuming, particularly if the question is not fully-formed or vague in some way. Try to resist the urge to participate in discussions relating to the question but simply listen, nod and then make a note of what the person is asking for. You should then make a point of placing the item into your in-tray and explain to the person who interrupted that you will get back to them by (you fill in the date or time). It is always worth having a reasonable 'by' time at the ready. This should follow your next un-booked period where you might reasonably address the issue. If it is too far in the future for the person with the request, you may find that that they seek some other solution which could work to your advantage but they will not reasonably be able to ask for you to look at it sooner as you have given them a realistic answer. E.g. 'I'll be able to get back to you next Thursday after my PPA time.'

You should then resume the task that you were completing prior to the interruption. The resulting action can be processed along with the other items in your in tray at the time you scheduled for processing. One of the main reasons people interrupt is that they are in the flow of solving a problem and they want their query dealt with straight away so as not to interrupt *their* flow. Not because it is actually an emergency or even an urgent task. Your flow is more important at this time and you should protect it. The interrupter assumes that the query will be dealt with more quickly if they are standing in front of you and this is usually correct because of the social pressure caused by their physical presence. However, once people get used to you not dealing immediately with their queries, they will probably choose other means to contact you or deal with the problem some other way.

Once the interruption is over, you are likely to be left with a variety of residual emotions. You are most likely to experience the feeling of relief, knowing that the interruption has ended. However, you will also be left with other emotions linked to both the nature of the request was placed upon you by the interruption and the manner in which you dealt with the person who interrupted you. You might have a positive reaction to a situation like this, for example if you provide someone with help or advice. Unfortunately, the feeling you are most likely to experience is guilt. You feel guilty because you have not given the person who interrupted you your full attention. It seems particularly unfair that you are left with this side effect as you did not request to be interrupted and on many occasions, may have implicitly or even explicitly asked to be left alone. The very fact that you are consumed with another action that does not involve the interrupter, means that no matter how much time you give them, you will never be giving them your full attention. But is this really wrong? After all the reason that they are interrupting you (with the exception of young children) is probably because they are consumed with some action of their own which does not involve you. If the person in question is a small child in your home, then the likelihood is they are feeling left out and tired of playing second fiddle to your work. If you know what I am talking about, this is probably the reason you are reading this book. Hopefully some of the advice will help you to spend more quality time with your children and family generally.

199

However, I must make the controversial assertion that your children are not the centre of the universe. They may of course be the most important things in your world, but in reality, the world your life should not revolve around your kids and you are doing them a disservice to create a situation which would cause them to believe this is case. If you say to your child: "Not now, I am busy. We will do X later when I am finished. Please don't interrupt me again", you are teaching your child an important lesson about boundaries. They may not be aware of it, but they too need unbroken time and space to complete their own work. You can lead by example by respecting their time and space and apologizing for interrupting. They will begin to understand: not everyone is available to them all the time. Perhaps the 'knockers' never learnt this message fully but most of us get there in the end. Give your children a head start and it will benefit you both.

Interrupters of the pupil variety may be treated similarly to your own child or adult interrupter, depending on the motivation for their interruption. They may want help, reassurance or simply attention. It is likely that none of the above are urgent, but all will be important to the pupil. As an educator, it is your job to train your students to be self-reliant, to use their initiative and have confidence in themselves. You also need to teach them about boundaries. In the same way you would not allow a child to eat sweets before bedtime, you should not allow them to constantly interrupt. You are training them to have positive social habits and whilst they may not fully understand the reasons, it's for their own good as well as yours. It is possible that you may also experience some regret at not having chosen your words perfectly or shown some agitation which may have caused upset. This realisation alone can make you feel annoyed, which ironically gives you yet another emotion to deal with! However, it is important that you hold on to the fact that it is near impossible to respond appropriately to circumstances you did not foresee and interruptions are ipso facto unpredictable events. The best you can do is develop a system for managing them consistently, using the same language each time. This is best done when you acknowledge rationally that there is no inherent reason for guilt in not allowing interruptions.

In addition to potential feelings of guilt and regret, you will also need to contend with range of emotions which result from whatever news was brought into your room. If you have any particular feelings about the person themselves, these feelings maybe nothing to do with what they said, but simply caused by their sudden presence in your life. This particular side-effect of interruption is the most insidious and difficult to remedy. Residual emotions will affect your sense of well-being making it very difficult to resume a state of flow. Emotions are the interrupters which keep on interrupting, reappearing in your mind every time you feel yourself beginning to refocus. If you have ever read 'The Power of Now' by Eckhart Tolle, you will be familiar with the concept of recognising these emotions for what they are: imposters. The best solution is just practise allowing them to come and go. Try to remember, these emotions are not yours they were thrust into your life by an uninvited guest; you do not need to receive them and certainly should not be maintaining their life source. Expel them alongside the uninvited guest and get on with whatever it was you were trying to achieve. I promise that with practice you will get much better at doing this, although I understand it may seem daunting at first. If meditation is not your thing, try reading *The Life Changing Magic of Not Giving a F*c** by Sarah Knight. It may help you to remind yourself that no one else dwells on thoughts of *you* accept in so far as your thoughts might relate to *them!*

If you have a particularly resistant thought or feeling, it can help to think of emotions as useful. After all, they are clues to a lesson; it seems that if work out the lesson and the feeling usually goes away. If it becomes a rumination, it doesn't have a purpose, so get rid of it. Save your time and energy and move on. Regret can be one of those particularly persistent emotions and can lead to you getting caught in cycles of retrospective planning. As it's obviously pointless to plan for the past, I recommend instead getting into the habit of taking what have you learnt and plan for future. Ask yourself what can I learn from this? Find an answer (which you should turn into an action point), put it on a post-it or on your to do list and then get on with the task you were about to accomplish.

In addition to the human interrupter, the digital world has introduced a whole host of other forms of interruption to compete for your attention complete with audio notifications. These are interruptions rather than distractions because whenever your device is with you, they can go off at any time and completely demand your attention. Whilst you don't need to act further, they have already taken your focus away from what you are doing and they have demanded your attention. Much like a new-born's cry, they can set off a whole host of involuntary reactions. The wonderful thing about these is they are entirely voluntary. Switch off the entire notification if you prefer, but certainly **switch off the sound**. The audio alert on your email works in much the same way. Thankfully old-fashioned ringing phones which cannot be switched off are disappearing but audio-alerts which are not kept in check are of the same breed. With all these audio-alerts, whilst you can avoid doing as the interrupter wants you to (answering the phone call, email, etc.), your attention has already been stolen and the damage done.

Some interruptions are emergencies. If you're a first aider, you will be interrupted by a multitude of potential emergencies each day. I realise in a school, someone has to have this qualification but I would suggest taking a long hard think about what it entails before you commit. I would go as far as to say that if you are a teacher who intends to do his or her job to the best of his or her capacity, being a first aider will only hinder this intention. If you are reading this book, you would possibly make a very *bad* first-aider. You know full-well that a great deal of tummy-aches or ice-pack requests are about the need for pastoral attention or even ploys to escape lessons. If you value your time may come resent the sheer volume of it such non-emergencies consume. But you can't have this attitude as a first-aider. You have to treat every single one as a genuine emergency - and this includes the attention, sympathy and paper-work for every single case. I know a school attendance officer who agreed to take a first-aid course as part of her role. It was a half day course. One day a pupil (one of the hundreds who visited her office on a weekly basis) arrived with a note from his Science teacher (also a first aider) requesting an ice-pack. It was administered and he was sent back to class. It later transpired he had broken his wrist and my friend having failed to diagnose this ended up being subjected to a tribunal, after which she lost her job. First aid is not to be taken lightly and therefore is not compatible with the priorities of a teacher.

First Aid aside, there are plenty of other 'emergencies' which interrupt our daily routines which are really just urgent problems. When you look at these more carefully you will be surprised at how many could have been prevented or the disruption minimised in advance. Many of those are recurring problems. If a problem occurs for the first time, you should always assess it and think: how can I prevent this happening again? The next step is to find the cause of the problem and then systematise a response for next time. If there is no system in place, then each time the event occurs, it's like Groundhog Day with the same old inefficient panic-response. Sometimes a problem may have never happened in our experience and most likely will happen very rarely or never in a teacher's career. However, for genuine emergencies like this, we are legally obligated to have well-oiled systems in place. Safeguarding is one, fire safety another, but there are plenty more, like the head bump procedure or 'lock-down'. Those systems are a great reminder of the way we should perform in our everyday lives. Imagine the carnage if a fire alarm went off and no one knew what to do. Not to mention the casualties. A policy is not a document on your desktop. Policy is what happens in real life. Sadly much of the time, urgent problems tend to recur in the same way again and again. Without a system in place, the problem becomes more than an interruption - it becomes disruptive. Meaning that it is at the extreme end of all four types of cost. Student answers back? Unless you wish to encourage this kind of thing, there should be a system for that. Photocopier breaks down. There should be system for that too. Student has a meltdown in the classroom? There should definitely be a system for that and whilst an interruption may occur, none of these events should necessarily disrupt the lesson. Of course most of the emphasis of your system should be on prevention of the occurrence to begin with, in much the same way we don't allow naked flames in the building. I would recommend you have your own personal policy-writing session in which you first identify your top ten time wasting occurrences. It is helpful to do this after a particularly unproductive day. Once you have identified what each of these occurrences are first consider how each of these situations may be prevented from happening in the future. Then consider how the situation can be dealt with in the moment, including an example script for the situation. Then consider how it might be resolved.

The process of reflecting on all the things waiting to steal your precious minutes, you will protect them more keenly. As Ray Dali argues in 'Principles', whilst we tend to go through life reflecting on events as though we have never encountered them before, eventually, the big picture afforded by experience will help us to see that each event is 'just another one of those'. Having a policy for each event of the same type will help save you time flapping, reacting and creating further problems as you deal with issues smoothly and swiftly. It also allows you to stay present in the activity you chose to do and to stay focussed on why you are doing it. Remember that whilst you can protect your minutes, you don't get to keep them. The time you protect from thieves *will* pass into nothingness and only its effects be they positive, negative or neutral are yours to keep. In this principle, we have reviewed the common time-thieves and how to combat unnecessary processing, entertainment media, switch-tasking, waiting, repetition and interruptions. Only Principle One will help you to stay focussed on the ultimate purpose for protecting your minutes to begin with. Once you have this purpose in mind, it will become your overarching motivator, empowering you with the innate will to combat the time-thieves like a mother bear protecting her cubs: I'm talking about your life's purpose.

EPILOGUE

AS YOU WERE, BUT WITH PRINCIPLES

'Someday isn't a real day like Monday or Tuesday; it's just another word for *never.'*

- Robert Herjavec

L iving your best life and being a time management teacher will be easy but it won't happen automatically. To begin with, it will require your intention and focus. You essentially need to re-write the rules using your own principles and the ones outlined in this book. Before you get started, it may help to get to grips with some of the challenges you are up against, so you can recognise the barriers when they arise and overcome them.

Our brains work in two very different ways simultaneously. The oldest part of our brain, sometimes known as the 'reptilian brain' (known scientifically as the limbic system) comes hard - wired with algorithms which tell us to seek pleasure and avoid pain. These are our default settings which come into play almost automatically in times of stress or when we encounter new situations for which we haven't yet established rules. When we pay attention to this part of our mind, we often refer to it as our 'gut'. Be warned: the 'gut' is not the mysterious guru we often mistake it to be. Our limbic system helps us to look critically at the world, encouraging us to spot danger everywhere. Whilst it keeps us alive and has enabled us to evolve, the downside is it tends to work against us when it comes to ultimate fulfilment. Incidentally, the reptile brain is responsible for the negative self-talk you hear when you're lacking confidence. Thankfully, the more reasonable prefrontal cortex developed later, enabling us to plan and see the bigger picture. This part of the brain is also responsible for our ability to connect to ever larger groups of people through language and abstract thought. It allows us to forgo the present in light of the prospect of bigger and better future gains. However, the two parts of the brain aren't built to work as a team, with one waiting in the wings whilst the better candidate tackles a particular problem. Rather, like two children competing for attention, they often try to act at the same time and this can lead us to live in conflicted and inefficient ways. We just need to be aware of where both the voices are coming from so we can pay attention to the correct one (rather than whoever is shouting loudest).

Consider the enthusiastic, pleasure-seeking friend you knew in college, who was always the life and soul of the party whilst you were wading through education policy. In all likelihood, she continued following her limbic system which served her so well in the past to the point where he looks around and finds she is dissatisfied with everything around her. Those key value areas we discussed in the previous chapter will likely be failing. Having neglected the forward planning, relationship-focussed part of the brain, she hears it now as an alien voice, telling her what she should or shouldn't do. Her 'gut' tells her it is too late to do anything about it now. She is too late. No matter how convincing the gut is – it is wrong. The problem is, her underdeveloped prefrontal cortex is the only part which can help her appreciate what can really be achieved in the next year, a month, an hour, a minute and she is not in the habit of paying attention to it.

I am guessing you are quite different to your pleasure seeking friend. Just the experience of reading this book has raised your awareness above the limbic cries and helped you to gain perspective on what is important. Hopefully this process has helped you to clarify your vision and principles and given you the tools to dedicate your time to only those tasks which can help you to fulfil your purpose. It is up to *you* to identify your wider purpose as a human being and those tasks which will help you to meet this purpose. Remember what Covey tells us: '*the main thing is to keep the main thing the main thing*'. The great thing is that once you have made your values clear to yourself, and identified principles and a vision to accompany this, it becomes more evident from your feelings when you stray away from your purpose. To live in a way which is not in line with our purpose requires us to adopt a kind of self-imposed numbness which often surfaces as 'guilt' and to avoid it requires 'escapism'. Recognise that low-level feeling of guilt for what it is: an indicator that you are not living in line with your purpose. Living against your purpose consumes your energy like the background drain of an open app on an electronic device. But now you recognise it, you can shut down the power-draining apps and work much more efficiently on the core program.

Once you have established your purpose as a human and drawn a nice thick black line around your 'work box', for one third of your time: you are a teacher. Principles Two - Ten will help you to cut the small stuff and go ahead and facilitate learning. Regardless of where and how you achieve this purpose, learning and enabling others to learn is an essential prerequisite of our human condition as we know it. It exceeds the bounds of a job role drawn up by a particular employer and can be deeply satisfying and ultimately the most rewarding thing you can do with your life. The principles in this book have centred on recognising and making the best use of your precious resources: particularly time, energy and money. As you have seen, these resources are closely related. Hopefully you appreciate by now that of the three, it is irreplaceable time which takes precedence: if you address how you use your time, the other two commodities will pay dividends. You need to differentiate between 'busy-work' and your life's work. You have the best job in the world - and now you have the chance to actually get on with what you set out to do. Get to work and make your life amazing!

A NOTE ON THE AUTHOR

Roberta Learner lives in West Sussex with her husband and children. She has spent her teaching career in the State and Private Sectors, working as a successful Senior Leader in both Primary and Senior Schools. She earned an MA in Education Leadership and Management for which she conducted research into to effective communication for Educational Leaders. The author enjoys writing as an author and copy-writer and owns a small company selling bespoke poetry and personalized gifts. Roberta began writing as 'The Life Long Learner' under the pen name R.J. Learner in 2016. 'Time Management Teacher' is the first book to be published in this series.

Printed in Poland
by Amazon Fulfillment
Poland Sp. z o.o., Wrocław

62475811R00125